how to
carry
what can't be
fixed

how to carry what can't be fixed

A JOURNAL
FOR GRIEF

MEGAN DEVINE

sounds true
BOULDER, COLORADO

Sounds True
Boulder, CO 80306

© 2021 Megan Devine

Sounds True is a trademark of Sounds True, Inc.

This book is not intended as a substitute for the medical recommendations of
physicians, mental health professionals, or other healthcare providers. Rather, it is
intended to offer information to help the reader cooperate with physicians, mental
health professionals, and health providers in a mutual request for optimum well-
being. We advise readers to carefully review and understand the ideas presented and
to seek the advice of a qualified professional before attempting to use them.

Published 2021

Cover and book design by Karen Polaski

Cover image and illustrations ©2021 by Naya Ismael

Printed in South Korea

ISBN 978-1-68364-370-8

10 9 8 7

Into the darkness they go,
the wise and the lovely.

Edna St. Vincent Millay

CONTENTS

INTRODUCTION

Finding Your Way with This Book (and Your Grief)

W e have this idea that there are only two options in grief: you can push yourself through to the other side, so that grief is over and done and you're "happy" again, or you can stay "stuck" in grief, locked in a dark room, alone, wearing sackcloth and rocking in a corner.

It's like a pass/fail test for the human heart.

With all the information out there on healing your grief, putting the past behind you, and harnessing the power of positive thinking, it can seem like everyone thinks your grief is a problem to be solved. The thing is, treating grief like a disease isn't going to make it better.

Grief isn't a problem to be solved; it's an experience to be carried.

If you're going to survive your grief, you'll need to find ways to inhabit grief—to live between those two extremes of "all better" and "hopelessly doomed." You need tools to build a life alongside your loss, not make that loss disappear.

As impossible as it might seem, you *can* survive your grief. It won't be all sunshine and roses, and it's not going to be easy. Everything I offer in this workbook is meant to help you come into relationship with grief, to help you learn how to carry it, and most of all, to help you come to yourself with kindness—for all you've had to live.

HOW IT WORKS

This journal is a place to tell the truth about your grief—all of it. It's a place to let grief stretch out, take form, and be as loud, long, bad, painful, melancholy, sad, and sweet as it wants to be, without anyone trying to pretty it up or rush you along. It's a place to note even the beautiful parts, and to explore the things that make your grief even the tiniest bit easier on you. On the page, everything is welcome.

You'll find writing and drawing prompts that go beyond "tell us about the funeral," and messages of encouragement from other grievers that are decidedly not cheerleading. It includes checklists and interactive comics to complete, secret love notes to write, and handy customize-and-cut-out sections to help you educate well-meaning friends and family. (Many of these are also available as downloads. Check the resources section at the back of this book.) There's even a section of scripts you can copy to help you navigate awkward conversations.

This journal also acts as a daily anchor. Circling back to the prompts, quotes, and exercises gives you something to do, every day, inside your grief. When life feels wholly overwhelming, those touchstones are important.

NOTES ON RESISTANCE

In my own early months of grief, I felt resistance to anything that promised to make my grief go away. Maybe you feel that way too. Nothing is going to take your grief away. Not this workbook. Not any resource. The removal of grief is not what we're going for. Instead, we're looking for companionship, acknowledgment, and the tools to make all of this just a little bit more gentle on your heart and your mind. I want to help you build on what you already know of yourself, find the love that remains, and follow it forward into all the life that is to come.

If you find yourself resisting any of the practices or exercises in this book, you can always write or draw your resistance. Explore it. Sometimes it has interesting things to say.

My grief-related work relates largely to death, but you can use this book for other losses too. Because I don't mention every kind of loss in this book, there will be spots where you'll need to put on your translator ears, listening for the way the words relate to your life. It's also important to note that you might not love every single thing in this book. Different exercises work for different people. Take what you need and skip the rest. My hope is that you find enough to keep you company.

Let's get started.

This journal is meant to be written in, drawn on, carried around with you to serve as an anchor in a storm, and even hurled across the room when that seems like the right thing to do.

As we get started, a few basic instructions might be helpful. Use them or ignore them as you wish.

The charts, lists, and maps in this book are meant to help you understand your grief, and to help you learn how to support yourself inside it. No matter how many losses you've faced in your life, this is the first time for *this* loss. Be curious about your experience.

Keep in mind that you can revisit the exercises anytime. Like any natural process, grief will shift and change over time, as will your responses to this book's prompts. What you needed the first time you completed an exercise might be different today, or tomorrow, or next week. Everything is always a work in progress.

If you're unfamiliar with using writing prompts, here are some notes on writing:

- Set a timer. Really. You'll be surprised how that helps. Ten minutes is a good place to start.

- Keep your hand moving! Keep writing until the timer goes off.

- If you get stuck, write out the prompt itself. Repeating the prompt is like priming a pump that has gone dry: it may take some time for the words to start flowing, but they will indeed flow.

- Prompts aren't so much points of debate or topics to discuss. They're more like jumping-off places for your own associative and creative mind: let them take you somewhere.

- When you open yourself to write, the words will appear. They always do. Not always the best words, or the easiest words, but words do appear. The same goes for drawing, or any other creative practice. The more you show up to the page, show up to *yourself* on the page, the easier these things will come. Some days the words will pour out in a torrent. Some days they'll feel slow and ornery. What's important is that you give yourself space to speak.

Notes on making images:

- Whatever your favorite medium is in this moment, that's the one to use. Pencil, marker, crayons—it doesn't matter. If the thought of drawing freaks you out (and even if it doesn't), you can always use collage to create images. Remember, they're your images—there's no one right way to make them.

- To get started with collage, gather a stack of magazines, decent scissors, and some form of adhesive (glue sticks, tape, rubber cement, and so forth). Hold the prompt or exercise in your mind as you flip through the magazines, pulling out any image that calls you. Let your mind wander through the pages. You don't even have to like the images you choose. Sometimes things that repel you have a story to tell, too. None of this has to make sense, and none of it has to be "art." You might look for larger images that can serve as a background, and several smaller images to create the foreground or main image. Arrange and rearrange them on the page until you feel ready, then start gluing.

Translating your inner emotional experience into words and pictures is a messy practice. It's hard to speak the truth if you have to make it perfect. This book is the place for raw words and images: sketches, first drafts, impulsivity, and stream of consciousness. It's a place to try things out. What you create might not be pretty. It really, really won't be perfect. If you find your inner critic getting in the way, give them their own notebook to draw in. A little time-share in the psyche is a wonderful thing. Criticism can wait its turn.

This book is not a substitute for therapy or other medical or mental health attention. I encourage you to share the exercises and explorations in this journal with your therapist or other support providers.

PART 1

DEPARTURE

CHAPTER 1

The Story Begins

What does storytelling have to do with your grief? I mean, this isn't just some story you're living. You're here because you lost someone you can't live without. Don't want to live without. Packaging all that up into a story with a beginning, middle, and end—complete with the main character's transformation into someone even better than they were before—that's just not going to work.

In the reality of death and loss, stories can feel largely meaningless.

But there is truth and usefulness inside the classic story structure, especially that of the hero's journey. It lends structure and order to what can otherwise seem formless and daunting. The hero's journey begins with the hero living her life, happy or unhappy, typically more content than she is restless. And then . . . something happens.

A stranger arrives, or an army invades, and she loses something precious, or death destroys something she loves. There's a journey she must go on, and she does not want to go.

I bet you don't really want to be here either. Grief is not an easy road. And yet here we are, together anyway, about to embark. Even that reluctance is part of the path as a whole:

> FRODO I can't do this, Sam.
>
> SAM I know. It's all wrong. By rights we shouldn't even be here. But we are. It's like in the great stories, Mr. Frodo. The ones that really mattered. Full of darkness and danger, they were. And sometimes you didn't want to know the end. Because how could the end be happy? How could the world go back to the way it was when so much bad had happened? But in the end, it's only a passing thing, this shadow. Even darkness must pass. A new day will come. And when the sun shines it will shine out the clearer. Those were

the stories that stayed with you. That meant something, even if you were too small to understand why. But I think, Mr. Frodo, I do understand. I know now. Folk in those stories had lots of chances of turning back, only they didn't. They kept going. Because they were holding on to something.

Excerpt from Peter Jackson's *The Lord of the Rings: The Two Towers*

You're doing this work because you want something for yourself. Whether your grief is a journey or an adventure or just some horrid thing you have to live and you hate all travel metaphors, you still need a place to begin. Beginning your journal with something creative can help get you out of your thinking mind and into the deeper truth of your heart.

If you are the hero in this story that is more than a story, that surpasses all stories, what is your point of departure? Take note of your surroundings. Are you already in the dark woods, with the light of your lost life far behind you, or is it still casting a glow at your feet? Where do you begin?

Draw, collage, or write your response. If you're really stuck, start with "I need to tell you what happened . . ."

Living what you're living isn't easy. Telling the story is important. Now that you've got your bearings a bit, let's talk about the realities of grief.

WHAT'S "NORMAL"?

Because we don't usually talk about the realities of grief, most people aren't aware of the many forms grief takes. While your "symptoms" might feel weird, you're probably not alone in experiencing them. Normal grief covers a lot of territory.

Even if you've lived through grief at other times in your life, you've never had to live this particular story before. Your grief might show up in interesting or confusing ways.

In the list below, circle or underline any symptoms you've experienced. What else would you add to the list?

Insomnia

Physical exhaustion

Time loss

Confusion

Sadness

Anger

Clumsiness

Sleeping all the time

Anxiety

Nightmares

Intense dreams

Loss of appetite

Loss of interest

Feeling like you don't belong

Eating everything

Frustration

Sense of unreality

Loneliness

Memory loss

Stomach pains, chest pains, and other physical sensations

Trouble concentrating

Hard time reading

Short attention span

Restlessness

Hypersensitivity

Phantom aches and pains

Interpersonal challenges

Nothing has meaning

Everything has meaning

Inability to cry

Numbness

Mood swings

Crying so hard you gag or throw up

Everyday tasks seem confusing

Dark sense of humor

Screaming in the car

Crying silently

Feeling different from everyone else

Feeling short-tempered

Abandoning your shopping cart at the grocery story

Feeling immense love for everything around you

BODY AND MIND

Grief is a full-body experience. There's a reason you're so tired. There's a reason your stamina might not be what it used to be. There is a reason your focus is off and you find even simple things confusing. Your mind is trying to make sense of something that doesn't make sense. Your body is trying to hold an impossibility within itself. Your entire system is working really hard just so you can survive each day.

Use the space below to write about the ways grief has affected you physically and mentally. You might begin with the phrase "Grief lives in my body . . ."

Or, you might draw an outline of your body in the space below. Using words, drawings, or collage, map out the effects of grief, locating them in your body. Use words or colors to name different symptoms, along with arrows to point to where they live in your body or mind.

Go back to that symptom list if you need ideas to get started.

WHY IS MY BRAIN SO WONKY?

Cognitive changes are common in grief. Memory, comprehension, attention—they all require a lot of power, and you just don't have the energy to spare. Think of cognitive changes like this: Let's say you have one hundred units of brain power for each day. Right now, the enormity of grief, trauma, sadness, and loneliness takes up ninety-nine of those energy units. That remaining one unit is what you have for the mundane and ordinary skills of life, such as organizing carpools and funeral details. It also has to keep you breathing, keep your heart beating, and help you access your cognitive, social, and relational skills. Remembering that cooking utensils belong in the drawer, not the freezer, and that your keys are under the bathroom sink where you left them when you ran out of toilet paper are just not high on the brain's priority list right now. Using the pie chart below, map out how your one hundred units of brain power are currently being allocated. What goes in the 99 percent? What's relegated to that 1 percent segment?

Because grief affects your cognitive skills (such as memory and attention span), try using alarms and sticky notes to help you keep track of details. Cover the entire house in reminders if that's what you need to do. They won't help you find your keys, but they might help you remember other things.

THE DAILY FOG

Remember that much of the work of early grief is done inside your heart and mind, not in outward actions. That you have no idea what day it is, or can't remember when you last ate, makes perfect sense. That whole hours pass and you can't name things you've actually done is normal (even though it might be disconcerting). It's in those lost, seemingly unproductive sections of time that your body and mind are attempting to integrate your loss. The daily fog is almost like an awake sleep cycle. Your mind goes off-line so it can heal.

It might not seem like much, but tending to your physical organism—eating, sleeping, drinking water, and moving your body as you're able—is one of the best things you can do to help yourself withstand the fog. Care for yourself as best you can, and know that the fog of daily time loss will eventually clear. Yielding to lost time and allowing it to be, rather than fighting it, can make surviving grief a little easier.

Color the image on the following page as you surrender to the seemingly unproductive, but necessary, off-line time of your mind.

ACCOMPLISHMENTS: ONE DAY AT A TIME

Your mind, like the rest of you, is doing the best it can to function and survive difficult circumstances. Grief and the daily fog really cut down on productivity. Please try not to judge your current accomplishments based on what you *used* to be able to do. You are not that person right now.

Let's look at what you've made happen today. Just this day. Did you drink enough water? Did you brush your teeth? Those count as wins. Give yourself an award for just showing up. That's a big deal.

Label each of these trophies with something you did today, no matter how small. Color them in. Celebrate these tiny victories.

RULES FOR SURVIVAL

Grief erupts into life and rearranges everything. It's not an ordinary time, and ordinary rules do not apply. Things that used to seem easy become enormously hard. Just getting through the day takes more effort than you expected. When grief reduces your life to such a small circumference of survival, you need a new rule book.

In the first few months of my own grief, I had a list of survival rules—reminders to help me make it through each day—or each moment. Here are some of my rules:

1. Safety first. Distraught driving is dangerous: pull over if you're crying too hard to see, and don't start driving if you're already upset.

2. Drink water. Crying for months on end is really dehydrating.

3. Move your body in whatever ways you can. It won't solve anything, but movement often brings a little more peace-of-being.

4. Get outside. Being outside in a nonhuman world is a relief: the trees don't care if you cry.

5. Tend something. Clean out the garden. Brush the animals. Send a care package.

6. Read. Sometimes the right words can shift things a little bit.

7. Shower. Really. You will feel just the tiniest bit better. Same goes for any other tedious hygiene task in your home or with your body.

8. Eat. Even if it is only small doses of healthy, nutrient-dense food.

9. Do not turn your anger on yourself. Notice if you're angry. Call it what it is, but don't turn it on yourself.

10. Say no to more things. Say yes to more things. Think about what has a good chance of nourishing you and get yourself out the door to participate (leave whenever you want). Turn down things that are likely to exhaust you or make you feel you have to defend your right to grieve (if you go anyway, leave whenever you want).

Your most supportive rules or guidelines will come out of *your* own experience. You know yourself best. Use the space below to write out your own survival rules for the rough realities of grief. Borrow from my list or craft your own. Make a chart, or style up your list as a mini-poster. Then, take a photo of your list of survival rules. Carry it in your phone. When the day ahead seems too big to withstand, use the list to remind yourself of ways to get through the day.

CHAPTER 2

What If I Refuse?

Nobody gets excited about grief. It's not an experience you take on willingly. You're here, but you don't want to be.

While you can't undo what has been done, you don't *exactly* have to go through grief gracefully.

Acceptance is a common grief-related buzzword. It's the alleged magic end goal of grief work. In the space of this chapter, however, you don't have to accept anything.

Survive it, yes. Accept it, no.

NO, NO, NO

So much of grief literature talks about trying to find the gift of grief, or finding peace inside it. So much of our grief "support" involves looking on the bright side, holding a positive image, or otherwise putting a glossy sheen on things. While there's a time and a place for some of that, you can't rush it. There has to be space to fight against what's happened. There has to be space to say how overwhelming this all feels.

If you can't vent your refusal, there's not much room for anything else.

Don't underestimate the power of the word *no*. Two little letters. So much force.

There's something powerful about saying no.

On the following pages, start out by writing the word *no*. Write it small, write it huge. Write it again. Collage it. Draw the outline of the letters and fill in the space with all the things you refuse. Make a million tiny little nos all over. In whatever ways your no wants to be said, give it room on the page.

(PS: This exercise might bring up some stuff. When you're done making a page full of nos, use the next blank page to write what it was like to just say no. Then, take a break. Eat, rest, move your body as you're able, do something else for a while.)

SAFETY-DEPOSIT BOX

Sometimes grief can feel like a life sentence with no hope for parole. You might be afraid of what might happen to you, since there can't possibly be a happy ending. Naming your fears can help you find a little space around them. If you ignore them, they'll just get louder.

On separate scraps of paper, write down your current fears about grief, and what your life might be like inside it. What are you afraid grief might be like in the future?

Now, because they're *fears*, letting them run around loose can allow them to multiply. We need to strike a balance between naming them and letting them run wild.

To help contain those fears, take an empty envelope, decorate it as you wish, and glue it onto this page. You might style it up like a safety-deposit box, or a locking treasure chest, or some other protective containment system.

Once it's glued down, open the envelope and slide your fears inside. Each time a new fear comes up, write it on a scrap of paper and add it to your lockbox.

ATTACH YOUR ENVELOPE HERE

WANT	DON'T WANT

WHAT DO YOU WANT?

Now that you've allowed *no* to let off steam, and you've named your fears, you have a little room to explore what you want and don't want for yourself. You might think you only want the one thing you can't have, but there might be other things you want (and don't want) as you survive this loss.

Using the chart above, write in the things you want and don't want. You can list feeling states, actions, or experiences. For example, on the "want" side, you might write "to feel supported," or "to have time to sort their things." On the "don't want" side, you might write "I don't want to feel rushed." Set a timer—keep writing for ten minutes. (Go longer if you want!)

A SNEAK PEEK AT THE FUTURE

Take a look at the chart you completed in the last exercise. It's a tiny little glimpse of your right-now road map. What did you find? What things do you want for yourself? What feels nurturing, supportive, or necessary?

In the space below, draw a quick picture or write a short list of the things you want for yourself, right now, inside your grief.

Take a picture of it with your phone. Carry it with you. You might even set alarms on your phone to help you remember to lean toward the things you want, and to avoid or decrease the things you don't.

CHAPTER 3

Getting By with a Little Help—
Real and Imagined

Even though the heavy emotional lifting of this loss is yours alone, you can't get through it 100 percent alone.

Sometimes friends and family are amazing; sometimes they all seem to disappear. For many people, it's a mix of both. Even with the best support, grief can be incredibly lonely. It's important to look for sources of support wherever you can. Surviving grief is a long haul, and it takes team effort.

YOUR HALL OF ALLIES

Let's start with the good stuff. When grief makes the whole world go dark, it's important to know who you can turn to—to know who's there for you, emotionally and physically.

Fill the following picture frames with photos or drawings of your support team: friends, family members, animals, and therapists or other pros. These can be people you've known forever, or new folks who just arrived on the scene. This is your "hall of allies." Even filling in just one or two frames is a good start.

BORROWING MENTORS

It's not always easy to find people who get it. Grief can make the world feel lonely. In case you need them, here are some words from people you haven't yet met. They're all students of mine, brought together by grief, sending their love to you. (For more love notes, check the resources section at the end of this book.)

How quickly we learn to mother each other. It is too much to bear our losses on our own, too hard to depend on those who have not been where we have been: in the desert of despair, in the wild wilderness of grief, we are fellow travelers. Our path is easier because we share it. How can I not love you? I wish you peace. I wish you days suffused with light. If only we could throw our arms around each other . . .   *Love, Ann*

May you know through every difficult moment, through every day, . . . that you are seen, and treasured, supported, and loved.   *Love, Julia*

I wish for you days without stupid comments that leave you feeling judged or nauseous or gobsmacked at insensitivity or somehow just worse. I wish for someone to companion you in your crater in silence or silliness or snark, [whatever] you need at that moment. I wish for you a full night's sleep, void of panic attacks and flashbacks and sudden wakings

in the dark. A sleep full of dreams of love and grace, close with your missing one, dreams to carry you, buoy you until you can find yourself once more.   **Love, Nancie**

For you, I wish the safety to show that tender spot where love blazes for those you feel but cannot see. I see you surrounded by endless compassion, starting with the care you show yourself.   *Love, Steven*

I wish that in this place that you've been forced into, through no choice of your own, that you find others who not only understand, but can truly empathize with what it's like to have your heart cleaved in two. I wish for you to find a community, your very own grief warriors who will protect, encourage, and defend you.

Love, Hayley

I wish you patience for yourself, and for the world around you to show you some patience, too. I wish you cardinals, dragonflies, breezes, moments of peace—fleeting and lasting. I wish you all the signs you're looking for. I'm looking for them too.

Love, Mary

When you are consumed by your grief, when life has lost its meaning and its beauty, when going forward seems impossible: May there be light, even if it's the tiniest blip in the dark. May there be comforting arms around you, friendly steps beside you, and empathic ears to hear you. May you know that you are never again alone, and that if nothing else, you have a family of people who understand. Though we may not really "know" each other, we understand, and we are here. We are here. You are so loved.

Love, Tamara

I wish for you the presence of another person walking beside you, in whatever form lightens your load. A kind soul who looks at the truth in your eyes and asks you how you are doing—not just today, but in a week, a year, twenty years from now. Gentle hands that hold your heart carefully and tenderly. Ears that listen patiently to your truth, without judgment.

Love, Sarah

May the trees of your forest grove fold you into their loving embrace and hold you fast in their graceful limbs. They are caring souls, the face of natural kindness. May they come to know your loves, your sorrows, and your joys.　　Love, Michelle

The heart opens in sadness. I see your loss, your grief. But more: I see your heart on the page here. I see your heart, and mine opens to yours.

Love, Mary

How I wish I could hold you. I know I cannot do this physically but can only offer to hold you as best I can in my heart and soul. May the space between us and around us be blessed by love and compassion.　　Love, Suzanne

May you feel the earth beneath you in times you're staggering, unsteady. May the canopy of a starry night sky companion you in times you feel abandoned and alone. May you look to the sun on the horizon in times you need reminding: there's more life, though a changed one, ahead of you. May the flowing river's run to [the] ocean help you know your journey is yours to find and follow. It's your path to make meaning in ways of your choosing, in your time. May you know yourself as home, within and without.

Love, Alison

WORDS ARE MY CLOSEST FRIENDS

Sometimes the best allies are words, not people. Use this page to collect quotes you find helpful or meaningful.

YOUR GRIEF MENTOR: FINDING THAT GUIDING STAR

Even with the best of friends and family offering support, grief is difficult.

You haven't lived this loss before. It's hard to know what to do. It's hard to know what's possible, living without the one you love.

Especially when grief feels entirely disorienting (and other people just want you to get over it), you need a guiding star, someone who lives their grief in a way you admire.

Grief is everywhere. There are thousands of experiences and millions of examples of how people live inside it. Look around. Are there people who live their own grief in a way that encourages, inspires, or directs you? You might know them personally, or they might be a public figure. Even a fictional figure can provide a road map to follow.

Use the space below to write about your guiding star. How has this person affected you? What feels possible in light of how they've lived their grief?

Finding a mentor can be tricky. If you don't have one, write about not having one. That's important too.

EXTRA HELP: CREATE A BONUS, MADE-UP, EXTRA-PERSONAL MENTOR

Even the best of humans aren't available 24/7, and sometimes even your favorite people can't hold the whole vision of how to best support you. It's great to have an imaginary mentor on standby.

Draw or collage your fantasy mentor below. You might start with a person, then add elements of animals, trees, or even parts of the landscape, such as rivers and mountains. Anything can lend its support. You get to be as practical or fantastical as you'd like.

You might call this creation your patron saint of grief, or your grief-fairy-godmother. Take a photo of this page and save it in your phone so you always have this mentor with you. If you're extra into it, cut around the image you create and carry it with you (the back of this page is blank to make that easier). Make photocopies in different sizes. Laminate them. Make them into stick puppets. It's *your* mentor, so make them and use them however you'd like. (PS: It might seem silly, but making an imaginary ally can be incredibly powerful. Give it a go.)

CHAPTER 4

The Inside View

G rief itself is sacred space. Not necessarily "good" space. Not necessarily "bad" space, either. But it is a space set apart from normal life. You cross a threshold when you enter into grief. It's a place not everyone can go, even if they want to accompany you there.

MAPPING THE TERRAIN

The world can become very small when you're inside grief. Time, space, love, distance—they make a unique geography.

What does the map of your territory look like? What are the key features? Where are your favorite spots? What's the geography of your heart and mind?

Creating a map of your grief can help orient you to this new world. On the facing page, add things such as landmarks, points of interest, dangerous passages, and places of meeting or connection. You can map the past, present, and future all on the same landscape.

Here's my example . . .

This is dog wash island, where you died that day.

There were double rainbows over the farm at your memorial.

This is the place I found a pile of heart rocks. Way over there is the beach where the dog and I play, and for a moment, all seems right with the world.

Here is your spot in our bed that I avoid each night.

Here is the couch that used to be yours, but we brought it here when you moved in. Remember?

Here is my spot at the kitchen table, where I spend the early morning hours before the others are awake, staring at the snow.

Create a map of your world as you see it. (Note that you don't need to be bound by the rules of the physical world.)

how others see me

how I wish I felt

how I really feel

POINTS OF VIEW

Nothing brings out unsolicited advice like grief and loss. Having a hard day? Someone will tell you it's not that bad. Feeling especially sad? Everyone has an opinion on what you should do to make that sadness go away. People also make wild assumptions about how you're feeling and how you spend your time while you're grieving.

How you see yourself in grief can be entirely different from how those around you see you. Following the examples above, create a series of portraits to explore these different points of view. You can draw, paint, collage—whatever you want.

EXCUSE ME, I AM NOT MYSELF

In the early weeks and months of grief, appearing "normal" is tricky. For example, a cashier asks you how your day is, and you burst into tears. You have to pay the parking attendant but can't remember how to make correct change. You want to tell people *why* you're acting so strange, but you can't find the words. Sometimes, saying things out loud is impossible.

Use the stickers on the facing page when you're unable to speak for yourself. Stick them on your jacket, plaster them on the back of your phone—whatever feels right.

To make stickers:

Cut the facing page out along the dotted line.

On a copy machine (or using your printer's copy function), copy this page onto blank full-page sticker sheets (8.5"-by-11" sticker sheets are available at most craft and office supply stores or online).

Alternately, find the link to a downloadable PDF in the resources section at the end of this book. You can print directly onto blank sticker sheets from there. Cut around the outlines of each sticker.

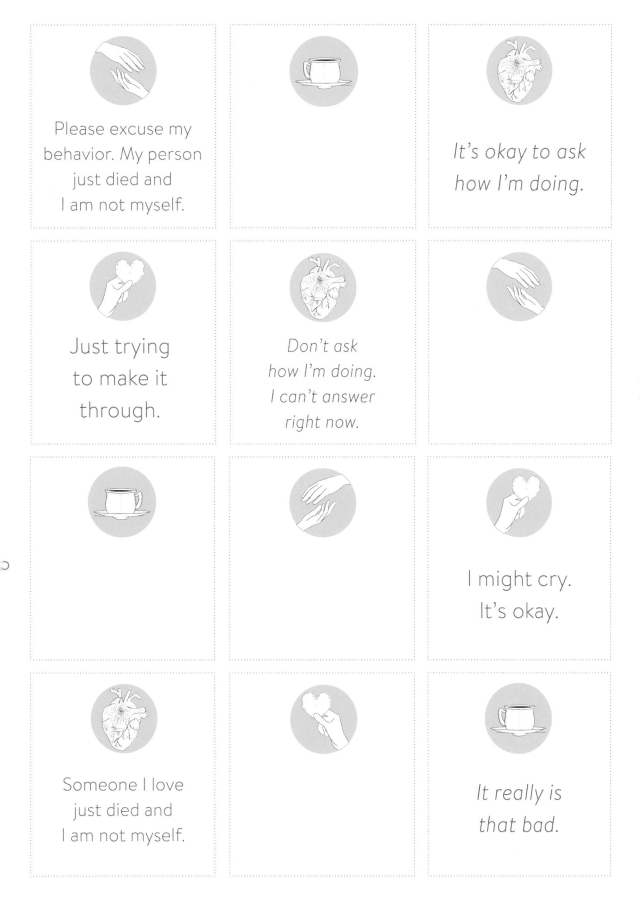

Please excuse my behavior. My person just died and I am not myself.

It's okay to ask how I'm doing.

Just trying to make it through.

Don't ask how I'm doing. I can't answer right now.

I might cry. It's okay.

Someone I love just died and I am not myself.

It really is that bad.

PERSONIFYING GRIEF

If you were writing fiction, you'd want to know the voice of your main character. You'd want to know the way they walk, the kinds of food they eat, how they comb or don't comb their hair. They would need to seem real. Similarly, your grief is a character: it has a rhythm and a voice. It is particular to you. Because we're going to be working with grief, let's find out who they are.

In personifying grief, we give it a voice. When it has a voice, it can tell us things.

Close your eyes. Take a few breaths. Pick up your pen. Take another breath, and on the exhale, ask your grief this question:

Who are you?

And then, wait.

When you see or sense an image—a being, a creature, a person—describe what you see. Don't tell us about it, let your grief actually speak. Write in its voice. (If you feel stuck, be outlandish: make something up. Play with the exercise. See where it goes. Give yourself at least ten minutes to write.)

Once you've written from your grief character's point of view, draw, paint, or collage your grief character in the space below, or on a separate sheet of paper.

If you'd like, take a photo of your grief character and upload it to social media with the hashtag #griefpersonified! This is one way to join with others who are learning to carry (and converse with) their grief. (See the resources section to find the link to the gallery to see what others have done.)

CHAPTER 5

This All Hurts

G rief is painful. We can find creative ways to connect with it, but it's still going to hurt. Once you understand that grief itself isn't a problem that needs to be solved, you might wonder if you're just supposed to be in pain for the rest of your life.

Well, no. And . . .

There's a difference between pain and suffering.

Pain is a healthy, normal response when someone (or something) you love is torn from your life. Pain hurts, but that doesn't make it wrong. It's going to be there until it softens, and it will do that of its own accord.

Suffering is different. Suffering is all the extra, added things that make everything feel worse. And unless suffering is interrupted or changed, it will just build into an even bigger storm of torment.

Things that cause suffering:

- Feeling dismissed or unsupported in your pain
- Judgment and advice on your grieving process (typically negative and unsolicited)
- Spending time with toxic, unhelpful, and exhausting people
- Excessive self-questioning and doubt
- Denying your real feelings
- Not getting enough food or sleep
- Punishing yourself for not preventing what happened
- Anything that depletes, exhausts, or aggravates you beyond the simple pain of loss

We can't remove the pain of loss itself. But suffering is, in large part, optional. Very often we can shift or change it, but first you have to learn how to recognize it.

DATE & TIME	ACTIVITY	I WAS WITH	BEFORE I FELT	AFTER I FELT

INVESTIGATION

The first step to reducing your own suffering is to figure out what causes it. You can do that by gathering some personal data. Mapping your interactions might seem a bit analytical, but the process can go a long way toward helping you identify, and therefore reduce, your suffering.

When you physically map out your days, the jumble of daily life starts to reveal itself as a series of somewhat predictable equations: *I sleep better when I take a walk late in the day*, or *Wow, every time I see that person, I feel really angry afterward.*

For the next week, use the preceding log to keep track of how you feel throughout the day in various places and in various social situations. Map your social interactions, how much sleep you've had, what you're eating (or not eating), and how you spend your time. You don't have to be obsessive with this log; broad sweeps of information can be as useful as minute detail.

As you fill out your log, be sure to note what helped you feel calm or peaceful too. Especially during very early grief, nothing is going to feel amazing. However, there might be moments when you feel steadier, less anxious, or capable of being gentler with yourself. If you find anything that feels less bad (in early grief) or, eventually, even a little bit good (whenever that happens), add it to your log.

Analyze the Facts

Once you've logged your interactions and feelings for a few days, go back over the results. Are there activities or interactions that consistently make you feel worse? For example, if your log shows that spending time with a certain person made you feel angry every time you saw them, that might be an instance of suffering you can erase from your life pretty easily: stop hanging out with that person.

Not every suffering-inducing item on your log can be avoided, but whenever possible, choose to avoid those things that increase your suffering. Doing so will make you more available to tend to your own pain, and will reduce the negative effect suffering has on your own heart and mind.

Use the following page to write out any observations you might have, given what your log shows. Pay special attention to things that could be changed in order to decrease your suffering.

SUFFERING ON THE SHELVES

While we're discussing suffering is a good time to talk about the grocery store. It's the number one worst place for grieving people. If you don't immediately think of your own reasons why, think about it: All those things you no longer have to buy for your person. All those healthy, "intact" families everywhere. Piped-in music that seems designed to make people cry. And those random acquaintances who decide *now* is the very best time to ask you intimate, personal questions about your grief—while you're just trying to get your bananas and get back home.

Take some time to color in the next page. You might create speech bubbles with things you love or hate to hear while at the grocery store.

HOW CAN YOU TELL IF YOU'RE DOING THINGS "RIGHT"?

When experiencing intense grief, it can be hard to tell if you're doing well or getting worse. Even when you map things out, it can be hard to separate pain from suffering.

EVIDENCE OF DOING WELL

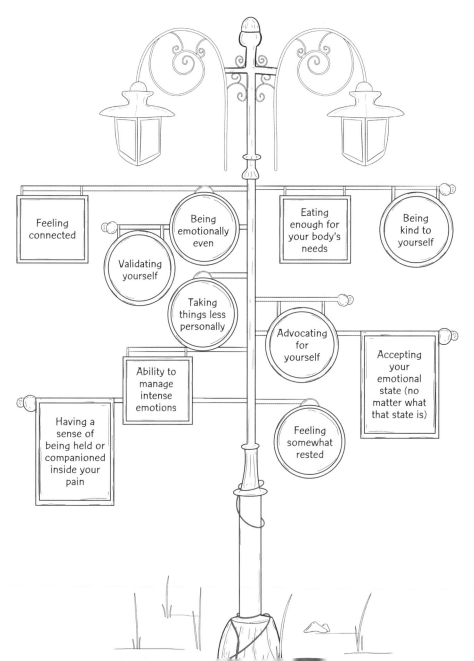

While each grief is unique, there are several broad indicators of doing well and not doing so well (aka suffering). Review some of the common signs on the lampposts below so you can tell the difference at a glance. Remember that you can be doing well inside your grief and still be in a whole lot of pain.

EVIDENCE OF SUFFERING

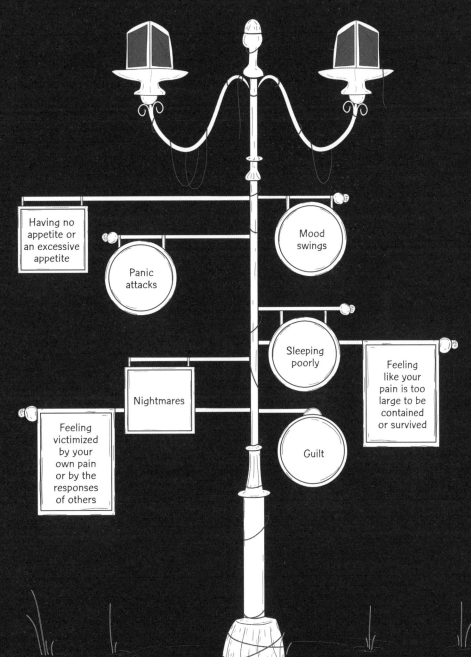

Having no appetite or an excessive appetite

Panic attacks

Mood swings

Sleeping poorly

Feeling like your pain is too large to be contained or survived

Nightmares

Feeling victimized by your own pain or by the responses of others

Guilt

Now it's your turn to explore how you're doing in your grief. On one lamppost, add signs that show you're really suffering (for example, not sleeping well, feeling extra irritable, and so forth). On the other lamppost, list signs that show

you're caring for yourself well (for example, feeling rested, being able to more easily ignore or shrug off small annoyances, and so forth). Reviewing the earlier sections in this chapter might help you generate ideas.

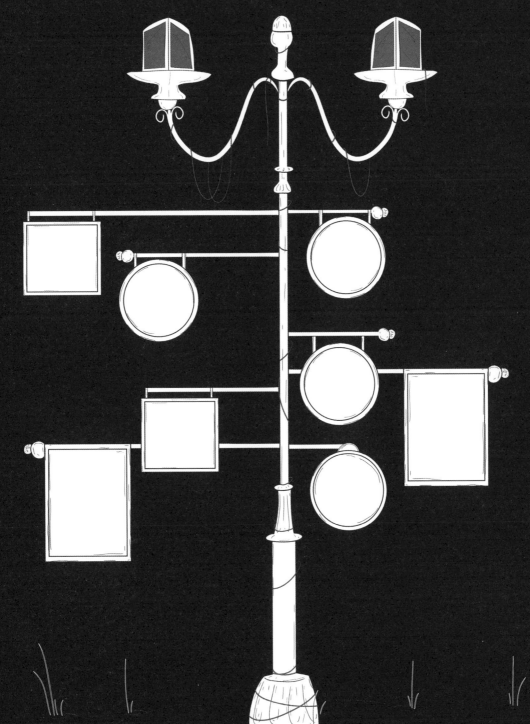

REMINDING YOURSELF

No matter how many times pain or grief has entered your life, *this* grief is unlike any other. Each new experience gets to unfold—and be tended—in the ways that best suit what hurts.

Use the information you discovered in this chapter to help you lean toward wellness and away from suffering. The knowledge you've gained won't make everything magically okay, but it can make things a whole lot easier on you.

To help you remember which things actually help you with your grief, choose five things from the first exercise in this chapter that make you feel more stable or calm—or that at least don't make you feel worse. Write them out again, in the space below. Draw, color, or decorate the margins around those five things. Make it fancy. Make it encouraging. If you think you'll need the reminder, include a note about how these things help. Take a photo of your list and keep it in your phone. When things feel horrible and you're not sure what to do, try one of these five things.

Just facing in the direction of wellness helps. Turn away from suffering when you can.

ADVENTURE
(of sorts)

CHAPTER 6

Rough Roads Ahead

Engaging with grief doesn't suddenly get easier. This is painful practice, this work you're doing. None of this is easy. The challenge is to stay present in your heart, to your heart, and to your own deep self, even—and especially—when that self is in pain.

Now that we've looked at some basic metrics for grief, let's dive into some tough topics.

Grief has some unfortunate side effects: anxiety, intrusive images, feeling like your emotions are too big to handle (sometimes known as emotional flooding), and sleep disturbances, to name a few.

Anxiety is a huge issue inside grief, so let's start there.

DON'T HIDE YOUR ANXIETY!

Lots of people feel a sense of shame around anxiety, as if they should be able to talk themselves out of it and remain chill at all times. If that's true for you, you might be tempted to pretend you aren't feeling anxious.

Unfortunately, it's not effective to pretend you aren't anxious. Hiding your anxiety makes it shoot out sideways. It makes your relationships feel strained and your mind ill at ease. We just don't lie about our anxieties very well—something always gives away the truth.

Anxiety is normal. It's yet another way your mind is trying to reorder the world after your loss. Please come to yourself—especially the anxious, fearful, terrified parts—with love and respect. Do your best to soothe your hardworking, over-worked mind when you can. Tell yourself the truth about your fears.

Try this: if you know you tend to feel anxiety, in the space following, write "I feel anxious more often than most people know."

Now what?

Take a breath (exhale, too).

In the space below, write just a few words on how it feels to claim your anxiety "out loud" like that.

Show It Some Respect!

Anxiety is information. It lets you know when you feel unsafe. It lets you know when you're worried about an outcome. It lets you know when things feel too big or too uncertain to handle. It lets you know you feel overwhelmed.

What it *doesn't* do is predict reality. Feeling scared about an outcome doesn't make that outcome more likely. It just makes you feel awful while you wait for more information.

In the space below, draw or collage a thank-you card to anxiety. Wait, *what*?

When you look at anxiety as a sign that you're under stress, not as a harbinger of doom, you can shift your relationship with it. Try saying thank you as an experiment. Thank your anxiety for helping you know when life feels big and uncertain. Thank your anxiety for giving you a chance to seek shelter and comfort, to take some space and slow down. Thank it for reminding you that it's okay to feel scared.

So yes, really—use the space below to draw or collage a thank-you card to anxiety. You don't even have to believe that this will help to give it a go.

Anxiety Log

If anxiety is a big issue for you, you might want to explore it a little more. Figuring out how and when you feel anxious can help you reduce anxiety's severity. It can help you soothe yourself when you do feel anxious.

If you aren't sure what sets off your anxiety, start logging the circumstances or situations that make your anxiety worse. It's just as important to take note of what happened on days when your anxiety was reduced, or nonexistent, too. What was different on those days?

DATE & TIME	ANXIETY LEVEL	WHAT MADE IT WORSE?	WHAT MADE IT BETTER?

Pattern Recognition

Once you've charted several days' worth of anxiety, look for recurring themes. For many people, anxiety increases when they're overtired, not eating well, or exposed to multiple challenges.

Are there patterns to your anxiety? When is it more noticeable? Are there patterns to the days when your anxiety is lower?

List the things you notice.

Anxiety Intervention

It's hard to come up with self-soothing skills when you're already exhausted and anxious. Looking back over the last two exercises (and drawing from what you already know of yourself), use the space below to create a short list of things you'll do to help yourself when anxiety starts to creep into your mind.

Bookmark this page, or take a photo to keep in your phone.

INTRUSIVE THOUGHTS AND IMAGES

The human mind is *amazing* at running disaster scenarios and replaying horrible events. This behavior is pretty normal inside grief, and you can't just tell yourself to stop. That's like telling someone to stop smoking, but not telling them what else to do with their hands. Intrusive thoughts can really fuel anxiety, too. To get relief, you'll need to replace the thought or image with something else.

On the following page, draw or collage a replacement image that you can call up in your mind any time the pictures or thoughts in your head are too intense. Choose one that you can use over and over again. It might be the comforting land-scape you'll find in the next chapter. It might be an image of someone you love holding and protecting you. What's important here is not the image, but the effect it has on you. Choose something calming and grounding.

It's going to be hard to wrench your mind away from anxiety-provoking thoughts and images. That's just how fear works; it's an addictive, persuasive mind-habit. When you notice that the thoughts and images in your mind are causing distress, draw your mind back to your replacement image. In time and with practice, doing so will become second nature.

Brain Break

Use this word search when you need to give your mind a little break from its mental torment. (For a key to this word search, see page 203.)

```
F  L  E  K  N  S  G  U  B  K  O  I  C  T  R  E  E  A  H  X  S  R  Y
P  T  E  A  D  O  J  L  I  A  W  F  O  U  N  D  H  E  A  R  T  S  A
E  S  U  P  P  O  R  T  T  E  F  A  O  K  N  I  G  W  B  C  V  E  L
V  L  U  E  R  D  X  M  L  K  E  M  H  N  E  O  P  N  J  S  E  T  C
O  T  V  H  I  N  E  O  A  P  S  I  E  W  S  D  N  T  U  Y  X  B  M
M  H  R  S  E  P  M  N  T  L  C  L  W  L  K  R  O  I  L  F  C  L  E
I  T  S  O  K  A  Y  T  H  A  T  Y  O  U  R  E  N  O  T  O  K  A  Y
S  D  L  R  U  L  C  M  E  T  S  W  Q  Y  C  S  I  D  B  I  E  N  C
B  C  E  I  G  W  B  C  V  I  O  T  V  Y  A  T  U  Z  N  E  R  K  J
J  S  E  L  U  E  R  D  X  T  U  Y  T  R  O  S  R  D  R  X  N  E  U
U  Y  P  K  O  I  C  T  R  U  S  U  W  C  L  Y  N  J  C  W  I  T  F
L  F  M  P  W  G  W  B  L  D  A  J  S  E  T  E  G  U  W  H  C  F  E
R  L  O  N  I  P  N  J  P  E  P  M  U  N  S  A  H  I  N  E  M  O  S
B  V  R  O  L  N  T  U  B  S  A  D  W  S  H  R  L  E  T  W  L  R  C
L  M  E  M  O  R  Y  F  O  B  U  A  H  M  N  S  O  P  N  J  K  T  Y
K  O  I  C  V  G  E  E  W  H  J  R  U  E  R  D  X  C  V  H  I  N  E
I  G  R  I  E  F  V  S  F  S  O  K  V  H  I  C  E  X  R  L  E  P  M
E  E  T  W  Y  G  E  C  E  R  S  H  R  S  E  P  T  U  E  R  O  X  T
D  P  N  J  O  U  R  S  S  I  R  U  T  R  L  E  A  W  H  I  N  V  D
R  C  V  H  U  O  L  L  C  E  B  M  O  I  C  T  W  R  S  E  P  M  E
E  W  S  D  N  W  N  E  X  R  C  O  N  N  E  C  T  I  O  N  A  Z  P
T  R  E  E  S  E  P  M  U  E  R  R  I  M  H  R  S  E  P  M  N  T  S
```

Focus on Your Breath (Sometimes)

In situations that cause anxiety or emotional distress, some clinicians and teachers recommend focusing on your breath, or on physical sensations in your body. But when you're dealing with anxiety related to death, injury, or chronic illness, turning your attention to the physical body can make things worse.

However, there is one breath-based action that can help.

Studies in both trauma sciences and neurobiology show that lengthening your exhale helps soothe the nervous system when it's agitated, as it is when you're feeling acute anxiety. This simple action stops the flood of stress hormones that triggers escalating anxiety.

When you're actively freaking out, remembering one simple direction is far easier than remembering a whole slew of other tools. So, when you feel anxious, remember this one simple thought: make your exhale longer than your inhale.

That it's simple is great. It's one option that is often under your control and always accessible. And it can help.

CONTROLLING YOUR FEELINGS

Grief is never going to feel good, but there are certainly times when the enormity of your grief is harder to manage than others. There's definitely a right time and a right place for giant feelings, and the grocery store might not be one of them.

So what can you do when your emotions feel overwhelming (such as when you're having a panic attack or just too many feelings at once) at an inconvenient moment? Focus on your surroundings, not your feelings. Calm your mind by counting or naming tangible things.

There is less chance of this practice setting off more pain when you focus on what is mundane, repetitive, neutral, and outside your body. Here are some examples:

- Count all the orange things you see around you.
  Name them.
- Choose a letter of the alphabet and name all the words you can think of that start with that letter.
- Count backward from 100 by 7s.
- List the names of all the plants and animals you know.

It doesn't matter what physical things you choose to focus on; it just matters that they're as mundane as possible, and that you can repeat the focusing process easily. You aren't trying to solve anything, you're just trying to help your brain calm down by giving it something to do.

If you tend to feel overwhelmed regularly, you might consider carrying a little notebook and a special pen with you just for this exercise.

Try It Now!

Don't wait for a meltdown before trying this exercise. Grab a pen and use this space to write down all the orange things you see around you. (Have an orange pen? Use that to make your list!)

Let's try another one! Write down all the words you can think of that start with the letter *K*. (Stop when you run out of room—or words!)

One more: List the names of all the plants or flowers you remember. You can draw them too.

A Go-To List for Tough Moments

Now that you've tried the previous exercise, help your future self out. In the space below, make a list of things you'll do when your feelings are too big for the environment you're in. Will you count things? Name things? Recite the alphabet backward?

Decorate your list. Make it soothing, simple, and clear. Add a short message that reminds you to find an anchor inside the storm of emotions. Take a photo of your list. Keep it in your phone. Use it anytime you need it.

Remember that turning away from your pain when your pain is too big for the situation is a kindness. It's a way to tend to yourself with love and respect. Get yourself through the flood of emotions as best you can, and come back to your pain when you have the resources and capacity to do so.

SLEEP ISSUES

Grief is exhausting. And sleep is the number one thing that will help you survive what you need to survive: it can help reduce anxiety, help regulate your emotions, and help you respond to life's challenges with more skill. The trouble is, grief can really mess with your ability to sleep.

There are certainly things you can do to encourage falling asleep, but as we know, grief doesn't follow predictable rules. Rest when you can, even if you can't fully sleep.

This is one area where your medical teams—both allopathic and integrative—can help. Talk with your trusted providers about ways to support more restful sleep.

Use this space to write down things that tend to help you fall asleep, and things that seem to prevent it.

THESE HELP ME SLEEP	THESE MESS UP MY SLEEP

Grief Nightmares

Though sleep is even more necessary during intense grief than it is at other times, nightmares about your loss can make sleep something you'd rather avoid.

Nightmares suck.

And yet recurrent dreams, or dreams that have you delivering the news about death over and over, are actually a healthy and necessary part of grief. Dream-state sleep is when our mind does the deep, heavy work of breaking down the reality of loss into absorbable pieces.

When you've had a grief nightmare, instead of analyzing it for hidden meaning, you might recognize it—and name it—as your mind trying hard to process loss. Something as simple as repeating to yourself, "My mind is trying to make space for this," can help calm your mind and soothe your nervous system when a grief nightmare wakes you.

Use the space below to write out a short list of things you'll do to help soothe yourself when a nightmare wakes you. If you sleep with your phone nearby, keep this list in it so it's handy.

CHAPTER 7

Rest and Restoration

G rief is a long haul. To get through this, you need nurturing, supportive sources of comfort.

You need places to rest. You need to get in the habit of asking yourself what you need. You need to know what activities refill your tank. And you need random reminders to help you stay rooted and grounded as grief dissolves and remakes your life.

This chapter has exercises to help you figure all that out.

A BLANKET FORT OF YOUR OWN CHOOSING

Let's go seeking comfort. Picture a landscape that feels protective and nurturing. Use the following page to create your landscape. It can be inside or outside, real or imagined, drawn or collaged. Add any items that feel comforting or give you a sense of love and support. If you're not sure where to start, create a blanket fort and go from there.

PS: Use this image as your happy place, even when you don't feel happy.

MESSAGE IN A BOTTLE

Sometimes an unexpected note can change your whole day, bringing a little bit of ease (or even humor) to a rough patch. Use the postcards on the following pages to write love letters to your future self. (Find a link to printable postcards in the resources section at the end of this book.) Special quotes and notes of validation or encouragement can serve as great messages too. Cut along the dotted lines, copy the pages onto heavy card stock paper, add your messages, address the cards to yourself, and give them to a friend to mail at intervals (or send them to yourself). You'll very likely forget what you wrote and be surprised at your presentience.

Some things cannot
be fixed.

They can
only be carried.

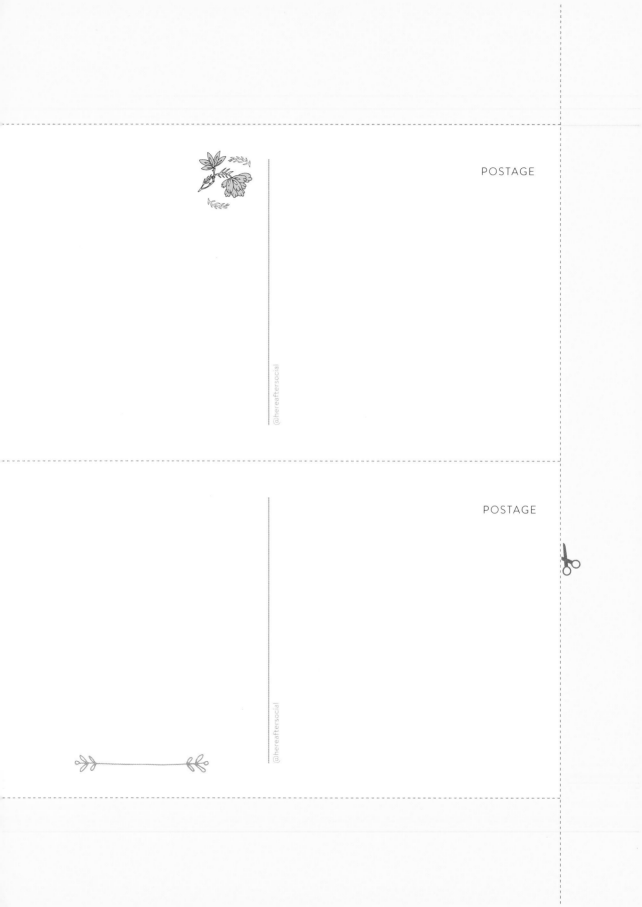

POSTAGE

@hereaftersocial

POSTAGE

@hereaftersocial

May there be a
tiny island of peace
inside your day.

POSTAGE

@hereaftersocial

POSTAGE

@hereaftersocial

AN IMAGINATIVE CHECK-IN WITH YOUR SELF

Your inner world operates as call and response: if you ask for an image, an image appears. Sometimes it's a bit clunky, and sometimes the image doesn't show up immediately, but an image always appears. Let's take a moment to check in with that inner world. (This exercise might feel a little woo-woo. Let's just go with it.)

1 Gather your favorite writing or drawing materials.
2 Take a moment to center yourself. By *center*, I don't mean feeling good or feeling ready, but being here. Take a few breaths.
3 Ask yourself this question: What is the condition of my heart?

Give the question some space. Wait for an image. The inner eye is not a fast-food joint; it might take a little time. If nothing seems to appear, ask again. Wait for a response. Let images arise without trying to manipulate or change them.

A visual image may appear. The imagery might be a literal heart, but the mind usually plays with metaphors or symbols. It might be a landscape, or an object, or a place or scene. It could also be a color, or a felt-sense, rather than a picture. The image that responds is the story of your heart, now, here.

Use the space below to describe what you see or sense. Spend some time with it. If it's an image, describe what it looks like. If it's a sensation or feeling state, describe that. Don't rush. Really explore what comes up. What is the condition of your heart?

You might be surprised by what responds, or by what you see. The image or sense may or may not be comforting. However, sometimes even an accurate portrayal of wreckage can be a relief.

When you feel you've described or drawn what you see or feel in enough detail, take a step back.

What's it like for you to see the condition of your heart?

Let your response fill the page.

IN CASE OF EMERGENCY

Fill the blank cards in the case with notes from friends, special quotes, and important reminders to yourself. When things feel bleak, close your eyes, circle your hand over the page, and let your finger drop through the "glass" to choose a message.

If you'd like to take it further, make a physical "in case of emergency" box by filling a shoebox or fancier container with notes from friends, quotes, and messages to yourself. Pull out a card when you need a little support.

A REAL SELF-CARE MENU

A social media search using the term "self-care" will result in lots of spa-day suggestions and imagery. Spa treatments can be lovely, but as a representation of what self-care might look like, they offer really limited options. Those spa-day suggestions presume that everyone feels nurtured and restored by a good pedicure and imply that the world can be made right with the correct facial followed by the perfect juice blend. Those frequently suggested ideas for self-care also presume a level of wealth or access that not everyone shares. You need better options.

Good self-care options help you rest and recharge when you feel depleted. Regular self-care can keep you from becoming entirely depleted, too. As educator Kate Kenfield suggests, good self-care helps you regroup so you can participate in life in the ways you most want. It lets you respond to challenging situations with skill and kindness. It lets you show up and keep going.

Sustainable self-care is more of a practice than a one-off event. When you have a menu of options to choose from, choosing to care for yourself becomes that much easier. Figuring out what really feels like self-care *before you need it* is a great gift to yourself.

Here are some ideas for your self-care menu that go beyond spa dates:

- Get in the habit of asking yourself what you need. One day, it might be physical movement. Another day, it might be time and space to reflect on and explore your emotions. You won't know unless you ask.

- Seek tactile comfort, such as a massage, a hot bath, or a warm pair of socks.

- Witness or participate in something playful: take your dog to the beach, watch videos of otters, do the most ridiculous dance you can think of . . . anything that might induce a bit of goofiness.

- Go somewhere beautiful. Make a short list of places to choose from, such as specific art museums, cathedrals, arboretums, or public gardens.

- Give yourself regular time to create. Gather your favorite art supplies in one box so you don't have to go looking for them when you need them. Even a few minutes of drawing and doodling can help you slow down and decompress.

· Connect. Time spent with the right people can refill your tank. Make a list of friends you can reach out to in person and online. Remember that different people are good at different things: one friend might be great when you feel sad and need someone to listen, whereas another friend might be better when you're restless and need some kind of adventure.

Use the lines below to add your own ideas.

_____

_____

_____

_____

_____

_____

_____

_____

_____

_____

_____

_____

TIME-TRAVEL SELF-CARE

If you have to do something hard—such as meet with your lawyer, or pick up ashes, or get through an anniversary—set up something nurturing and comforting for after the event.

When you're diving into big emotional activities, you also might set a timer so you have a stopping point. For example, set a timer for ninety minutes before you sort through the death-related paperwork. It might seem silly, but giving yourself a concrete end point can help you manage tough emotional events.

Use the ideas on this list to make things easier for your future self, and use the blank lines to add your own time-travel self-care ideas.

- Set up all the things you'll need for a walk: jacket, shoes, headphones, house keys. Set a timer before you begin a challenging task. When the timer goes off, go for a walk.

- Ask a friend to text you when you expect the event to be over. Give them a specific time, and ask them to set an alarm so they remember to check in.

- Before you leave the house, set up your tea kettle, your favorite mug, and some delicious tea. Fold your comfiest clothes, and set them nearby. When you get home, all you have to do is heat water and change clothes.

- Arrange to meet friends for a movie after the event. Tell them you might not want to talk, but you'd love their company.

- Ask a friend to keep a candle lit for you during the event itself. Ask them to text you a photo of their candle a few times during the event. Knowing someone is out there, thinking of you, can give you just enough to make it through.

KINDNESS IS EVERYTHING

What you're living isn't easy. Treating yourself kindly won't change grief itself, but it will make things easier on your mind and your heart.

The tricky thing is . . . finding kindness for oneself is the hardest thing to do. We can offer kindness to even the most hard-hearted individuals in the world, but kindness for yourself? No. Nope. *I can't be kind to myself. That's letting myself off too easy.*

If you're feeling an intense aversion to the idea of kindness for yourself, you are not alone. It's hard for everyone.

Because kindness for self is so hard to practice, it's important to have daily, tangible reminders. Try kindness on, just for a few minutes. Turn toward it, even if you can't make it all the way there. Turn yourself in the direction of kindness. Hold on to it.

What would kindness for yourself look like today? In this moment? Write your answers below.

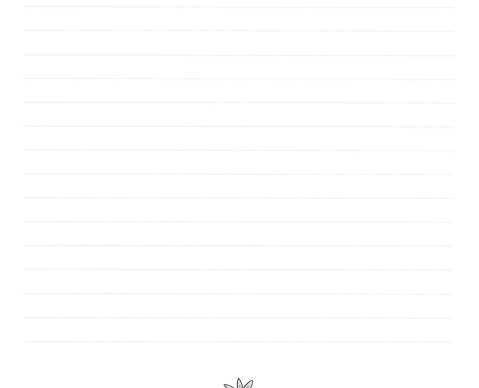

Grief requires kindness. Self-kindness. For all you've had to live.

Some Self-Kindness Suggestions

Kindness for self might be allowing yourself to sleep as much as you need to, without yelling at yourself for it.

It might be saying no to a social engagement.

It might be turning the car around right after you've arrived in the parking lot, having decided that getting groceries is just too much for you to bear right now.

It might mean cutting yourself some slack, backing off the demands you place on yourself.

It might mean pushing yourself sometimes, taking yourself out of the softer nest of distraction and exploring the bigger landscape of pain.

What kindness looks like will change, but your commitment to it can remain constant. That's where your safety is—knowing you won't leave yourself. Knowing that, to the best of your ability, you'll come to yourself with kindness. In a world that feels bizarre and shaken, your commitment to self-kindness offers some stability.

SELF-CARE MANIFESTO

If you created your own manifesto of self-care, what would it include?

In therapy, I often remind people of the airplane safety analogy: in times of trouble or danger, put your own oxygen mask on first before you try to help others. Inside your grief, you have to put yourself first. To survive, you have to become fierce about caring for yourself.

A manifesto of self-care is a road map for survival. It's shorthand and course correction for when you feel overwhelmed and lost in your grief. It's support and encouragement to stay true to yourself, to follow your own needs when the outside world insists that you do things its way. It helps you choose kindness over self-flagellation.

Perhaps the name *manifesto* seems inflated and self-important. But seriously—being fierce about your own needs, putting yourself first, insisting on making space for what makes this better, easier, gentler—nothing else is more important.

A manifesto of self-care can be as short as two words: practice kindness. It can also be a love letter to yourself or a list of ten or so things that are important to remember. Create your own manifesto of self-care on the following page. Style it up. Make it pretty. Make it fierce. Take a photo of it. Keep it in your phone. Make it the background image on your laptop. Stick it on your fridge. Post it everywhere.

May you, to your own sad self, be kind.

CHAPTER 8

The Gifts and Perils of Distraction

G rieving people can't win. If you show your feelings, people say you're "too emotional" and need to move on. If you don't show your feelings, you're in "denial" and need to face the truth. It's really no wonder that most people keep their grief to themselves.

The thing is, you're not meant to withstand the full force of grief all at once. It's just not possible. There have to be times when you can look away, avert your gaze, and numb out.

When grief is new,* you're inside that intense emotional wound every second of every day. Pain is everything: it's exhausting and all-consuming.

Some days, some moments, you're able to hold your gaze on your own broken heart, and some days, some moments, holding that gaze feels impossible.

Having compassion for yourself in those moments when you witness your own pain includes being kind enough to drop your gaze when it gets to be too much. It's okay to turn away when you need to.

It's okay to feel yourself numb out. Numbness is part of grief. The need to avert your gaze is normal when loss has you reeling. It's healthy, even. It's a kindness. Kindness counts.

Finding good distractions can be tricky. It's not like your loss will "go away" while you're at the movies (actually, movie theaters are among the worst places for distraction). *Good* distractions let you shift your focus, allowing something else to take center stage for a bit. Good distractions give you a little breathing room. If there's anything that gives you even a moment's relief or respite, move toward that.

As a regular practice, you can check on the condition of your heart to help you know what you need. Each day—each hour—will be different. Before you

---

*Define "new" for yourself.

dive into a bunch of checked-out activities, check in with yourself. Ask yourself what you need. That way you have a better chance of getting what you're actually looking for. Checking in on your checking out also lets you know if your go-to distractions are causing more harm than good.

PLANNING IN ADVANCE

Creating a menu of distraction options before you need them is a great act of self-care and kindness. A little bit of effort can go a long way.

On the list of examples below, highlight the things you've tried. Circle the ones you might be willing to try. Add additional activities on the lines below.

- Exercise
- Watch TV
- Listen to a new podcast
- Draw mandalas
- Take a nap
- Volunteer
- Bake for a friend
- See a movie
- Go to the beach
- Draw temporary tattoos on yourself
- Conquer a complicated recipe
- Walk in the woods
- Play video games
- Read a fantasy novel
- Browse a bookstore
- Try a new sport
- Take a class in something you've never done
- Take an art break: go to a gallery or museum

- Work in the garden
- Take a road trip
- Tackle a home-improvement project
- Practice a new language
- List all the plants and animals you can think of
- Spend time looking for goodness or positive things
- Go on a beauty scavenger hunt (find thirty tiny beautiful things)
- Read the entire archives of a blog you like

_____

_____

_____

_____

_____

_____

_____

RESULTS OF MY DISTRACTIONS

Look back on the exercises you completed in chapter 5. Consider all the activities you logged that might qualify as distractions or emotional breaks. What distractions do you tend to use? How do you feel when you use them? How were you hoping to feel? Did you get what you wanted out of them? Let's find out.

Maybe for today's "emotional off-switch" you went for a run while listening to a podcast. You were hoping the run would help decrease your anxiety and make you tired enough to sleep tonight. After the run, you definitely felt tired, and at least while you were running you didn't notice any anxious thoughts. If you map that out, it would look like this:

I FELT	Anxious and tired
I WANTED	Less anxiety and more sleep
I CHOSE	Ran 3 miles, listened to a fiction podcast
THIS HAPPENED	Definitely tired, had a break from anxious thoughts

Sometimes you won't get what you want from an activity. Maybe the podcast you chose to listen to had a surprise grief plot line. Maybe eating an entire pizza while you binge-watched TV felt great in the moment, but it completely trashed your sleep. You might still choose those activities for their short-term relief, but understanding the potential consequences lets you make more informed choices. You might also realize, for example, that running hurt, and that you decided to run more because you were punishing yourself. Mapping things out can show you where checking out can be a warning sign.

Map your go-to emotional off-switch activities here:

I FELT	_____
I WANTED	_____
I CHOSE	_____
THIS HAPPENED	_____

HOW MUCH IS TOO MUCH?

The siren song of numbness can be strong, because grief is intense. Looking for relief is healthy. Living full time in la-la land is not. Let's take a close look at your usual distraction activities. How much is too much? Let's look at two examples. Then, in the blank space below, map some of your own usual activities. Use this to help you navigate between helpful distraction and completely checked out.

ACTIVITY	Movie marathons
HOW OFTEN DO I DO THIS?	All day, every day
WHAT'S THE RESULT?	I feel hungover at the end of the day: bleary and slow.

ACTIVITY	Enforced positivity
HOW OFTEN DO I DO THIS?	It's the only mind-state I allow myself
WHAT'S THE RESULT?	What do you mean? Everything is fine!

ACTIVITY	
HOW OFTEN DO I DO THIS?	
WHAT'S THE RESULT?	

ACTIVITY	
HOW OFTEN DO I DO THIS?	
WHAT'S THE RESULT?	

ACTIVITY	
HOW OFTEN DO I DO THIS?	
WHAT'S THE RESULT?	

ACTIVITY	
HOW OFTEN DO I DO THIS?	
WHAT'S THE RESULT?	

An important note: While giving yourself an emotional off-switch is important, some activities are dangerous. Please reach out for help if you find yourself engaging in heavy drug or alcohol use, self-harm, or reckless/dangerous behavior that puts you or others in harm's way. Check the resources section of this book for assistance. Help is available.

CHAPTER 9

Anger Deserves
Its Own Chapter

Anger doesn't get much positive airtime in our culture. Much like grief, it is met with deep discomfort: short doses of anger are fine, but anger needs to be moved through quickly, without much noise.

You're not supposed to be angry. No matter what's happened, you're just supposed to . . . stay calm. Don't make such a fuss. No sense getting angry at something you can't change.

But being angry is normal. It's a healthy human emotion.

Anger deserves to be heard—here in this journal, and out there in your life.

All emotion is a response to *something*. Anger is a response to a sense of injustice. It doesn't matter whether "fairness" is logical, or whether there's a reason something happened.

Of course you're angry: whatever has happened is unjust, and it doesn't feel fair. Of course you're angry about the weird, unhelpful things people say. That they have "good intentions" doesn't mean their words shouldn't bug you.

When you allow yourself to express anger, it's simply energy. It's information. In some cases, anger gives you the energy to face what is yours to face. It becomes a fierce protective love—for yourself, for the one you lost. Shown respect and given room, anger tells a story of love and connection and longing. There is nothing wrong with that.

When we suppress and silence anger, we suppress both the truth *and* our own vitality—our own fierceness for ourselves and those we care about. Meeting with your anger, honoring it, giving it space—all of these things are healthy. Give your sense of injustice and anger a voice. Connect with it, channel it. It's part of you, and it deserves space to exist.

OF COURSE YOU ARE

When it's okay to talk about anger, it has a lot to say. In the space below, as quickly as possible and without thinking too much, write "Of course I'm angry."

Start there, and see what comes. Write for ten minutes, or until you feel done.

THE ANGER METER

Because a healthy relationship with anger is new territory for a lot of people, just recognizing your own anger level is a step in the right direction. Like all emotions, anger will ebb and flow, shift and change. Color in the anger meter below with today's anger level:

Tomorrow, fill this one in:

Create your own anger meter to help yourself do a check-in on a regular basis. Getting to know your anger level is a great place to begin a new relationship with this much-maligned emotion.

LOCATE YOUR HOT SPOTS!

Anger comes in many forms. What sets you off might be different from what sets off someone else. You'll find some responses that annoy a lot of people in the drawing on the next page. Cross out any that don't bug you, and use the space between those things to add your own. You might add phrases that make you angry, or situations that are inherently frustrating—like going to court, or calling customer service.

If all of this makes you want to throw this book, do it!
Just . . . aim carefully so you don't break something.

At least you had them as long as you did.

Everything happens for a reason.

You should be more grateful!

They're in a better place.

A PLACE TO BE ANGRY

Where is your anger today? Is it breathing fire alongside dragons, or is it smashing rocks on the side of a volcano? Maybe it's a Tasmanian devil whirling through the open plains. Maybe it's just out for a run, pounding outrage into the dirt.

Color the scene on these pages. Add yourself where you'd like to be today, doing whatever you want with your anger.

THINGS TO DO WITH ANGER

There are lots of ways to express your anger. Here are just a few examples:

Yell

Pound on things (safety first, though!)

Make discordant music (or listen to it!)

Paint (big or small, messy or intricate)

Exercise (move that energy!)

Lift weights

Vent to a friend

Start a movement

Stand up for someone

Stand up for yourself

Just do something with your anger, rather than try to subdue it. You're much more likely to use your anger skillfully if you acknowledge its right to exist.

Below, make a list of constructive things you might do with your anger.

things to do when I'm angry

SAFETY FIRST

Getting in touch with your anger can be scary. If it feels too big, lean on a trusted friend or therapist. It's okay to ask people if they're open to hearing your anger about a situation. Doing so lets them have a choice. If they say yes, they'll be prepared to really listen, and you'll know that they're willing to hear your anger without trying to rush you out of it.

Use the space below to list the people who might be able to hear your anger, and the places that might feel safe for you to express your anger.

Being angry doesn't give you license to harm yourself or someone else. Don't use anger as a weapon or as an excuse for aggressive behavior. Listen to it. Honor it. Respond with skill. Anger is information, not justification.

WHAT ABOUT RAGE?

Rage is a little different from anger. Rage is what can happen when anger is denied or silenced for too long. It's violent and destructive. That's why it's so important to give your anger a voice—to use it skillfully, rather than let it tear down the world

Anger is a tricky emotion. We don't talk about it much, which means it often has to get *really* loud to deliver its message. Fill out the anger pledge below to help you know how to honor, respect, and channel your anger.

The Anger Pledge

I, _____,

hereby pledge to honor my anger as a trusted source of information. It allows me to know when I feel I've been treated unfairly, and when my boundaries have been crossed. My anger deserves respect and space to express itself.

From this day forth, I will express and channel my anger through the following:

_____

_____

_____

I will use my anger to help fuel or create:

_____

_____

_____

I promise to use my anger with increasing skill as I come to know it, and myself, better.

SIGNED ON THIS _____ DAY OF _____ (MONTH), IN THE YEAR _____.

_____

YOUR SIGNATURE HERE

CHAPTER 10

The Vantage Point

L iving with grief isn't easy. Though much of your focus might be on surviving each day, it's important to take note of the progress you've made. Taking time to acknowledge your progress, and to remind yourself of what's important, helps make grief bearable.

Your pain deserves your kind, compassionate, simple honesty and care. Take a break from your exploration of anger to color the image below, then take stock of your surroundings once again.

REST STOP

Take a few moments to look back over the work you've done so far in this book. (Don't worry if you haven't completed everything. This book is not a test, and these exercises aren't assignments. Just look at what you've completed, and don't stress about what you haven't.)

Has anything developed, or has something become clear that you hadn't seen before?

What have you learned about yourself, or your grief? Has anything surprised you?

Set a timer and respond to these questions in the space below. If you get stuck, or need a place to start, try writing "I didn't think this would be so hard," or "I didn't know I needed . . ." or "I thought I would find . . ."

If you get really stuck, try writing "I didn't know . . ." and filling in the end of the sentence over and over again—as many times as you need to.

LITTLE LETTERS TO MYSELF

Staying grounded inside grief can be tricky. Big emotions, a flood of memories, irritating encounters—they can all knock you off-balance. Using the note cards below, write reminders to yourself about what's important, and what you want to remember, in times of hardship and struggle. You might include quotes you find meaningful, too.

Bookmark this page for easy access. You can also remove this page by cutting along the dotted line, then cut the cards apart so you can carry them with you or place them in strategic places, such as on your bathroom mirror or in your car—wherever you might find yourself needing a little boost.

BOUNDARIES ARE OUR FRIENDS (AKA: CIRCLES OF PROTECTION)

Grief can make you feel porous—like everything affects you (and not in a good way). Good boundaries—emotional, physical, and relational—help give you a sense of control over your own experience. Imagine yourself inside the circle below. Draw or write the things that help you feel centered (or at least, not stirred up). In the space outside the circle, draw or write the things that knock you off balance. For example, outside the circle, you might add "endless online scrolling" or "my neighbor's intrusive questioning." Inside, you might add "time in nature" or "creativity podcasts."

TOO PRECISE TO BE RANDOM: ON SIGNS AND SYNCHRONICITIES

A well-timed song, the appearance of birds or hearts or sudden messages, things showing up just as you've thought to look for them—almost everyone has a story of something happening in their grief that felt like a sign.

We don't often talk about this stuff. Such occurrences are the sorts of thing we share surreptitiously. Carefully. With disclaimers and explanations and vows that we don't actually believe in signs, because we are not flaky.

No one wants to be seen as flaky.

Whether these "too precise to be random" things are simply our brains making connections—which is completely cool in and of itself—or they hint at some larger mystery beyond what we see doesn't matter. What matters is the comfort or connection you draw from them.

Use this page to record your own collection of signs, dreams, and synchronicities that are too precise to be random.

A sign is only a sign if you choose it yourself: no one else
gets to decide what has meaning for you.

EXTRA-FUN ACTIVITY: BE AN AGENT OF SYNCHRONICITY!

Who left that big heart drawn in the sand for you to find? How'd that "I love you" note get on that bathroom mirror in the café? Sure, they were meant entirely for you, but how'd they get there?

Spreading little love notes is one way you can create a tiny spark of magic and connection for someone else. Use this page to brainstorm creative ways you can create messages for others to find—just precisely when they need them.

If you'd like to share your secret agent moments, take photos and share them on social media with the hashtag #tooprecisetoberandom.

CHAPTER 11

The Ultimate Boon

There are gifts that come with grief, gifts that come with being intimately familiar with loss. However, that doesn't mean it's a fair trade: your life that was in exchange for the gifts you now possess.

Maybe you have less tolerance for bullshit now. Maybe you've cut things out of your life that needed booting a long time ago. Maybe you feel adventurous or assertive, because the worst has already happened and you feel a little invincible. Maybe life feels more intense, and not in entirely bad ways. Maybe you *do* see more love in the world, through your new grief-eyes.

Though you'd trade all these gifts just to have your life back, grief isn't a complete dump truck full of doom.

This chapter lets you explore the gifts of grief—without the pressure to give up your grief to claim them.

THE 13TH GUEST

The number 13 gets a bad rap in Western culture. Friday the 13th is seen as unlucky. Some buildings skip the 13th floor, jumping from 12 to 14 (as if you can avoid something crappy by skipping a number). Fear of the number 13 has its own multi-syllabic psychiatric label: triskaidekaphobia.

Even fairy tales continue the anti-thirteen bias. In the original *Sleeping Beauty*—who was called *Briar Rose* by the Grimm brothers—the king and queen only had 12 gold plates, but there were 13 fairies. Rather than find an extra plate, they decided to exclude one of the fairies. Later retellings of the story made the 13th fairy into an evil witch, and her unacceptable nature was the reason she wasn't invited.

That theme of the ugly old witch shows up in story after story—sometimes she's a witch, sometimes a wicked stepmother, sometimes just an undesirable guest. Whatever she's called, the effect is the same: her presence makes others uncomfortable.

She's never going to get a spot on the guest list.

But in many of the stories, that old witch shows up at the party anyway.

She arrives, the 13th guest, bringing an uncomfortable blessing, or some kind of unsettling gift. Quite often, the gift she brings has something to do with death.

It's important to note that the 13th guest doesn't cause death, she is simply comfortable with it. She's not afraid to reveal her knowledge about things other people try to avoid.

No wonder she's not invited.

When you're living inside deep grief, you're consciously aware of the dark presence you bring to social settings. You might find yourself conveniently not invited to the neighborhood barbecue, or left off the guest list of your friend's wedding. No one wants a reminder of death to show up at their event. Who wants to think about death or disease when you're trying to have a party?

Or maybe you've felt self-conscious about your effect on others and decided to exclude yourself, first. After all, you have nothing to talk about but death and grief. There are no other topics. You don't feel very festive.

Either way, when you're grieving, it can be hard to feel welcome anywhere.

Can you imagine yourself in the fairy tale? Are you the old wise person who brings an uncomfortable gift to the party? How do the people around you see you? Are they afraid, superstitious, uncomfortable? Do you excuse yourself from the party, rather than bring what you know to the table?

In the space below, write about yourself as the 13th guest.

GET OUT OF (SOCIAL) JAIL FREE CARD!

When you do get invited to a social event, it can still feel awkward: you don't want to be alone, but you don't really want to be around "normal" people, either. If you're struggling with how to respond to an invitation, one of these cards may help. Cut them out and distribute as needed (especially when a little dark humor or snark seems in order). Customize the blank cards to suit the occasion.

MY NEW KNOWLEDGE

While intense loss isn't a prerequisite for life wisdom, some things do get thrust into sharp relief inside grief. Maybe you have more empathy for others. Maybe you state your boundaries more clearly than you did before your loss. Maybe your loss has brought new insight into relationships, or to the state of the world.

What have you learned as a result of your loss? List what you've gained below.

WHAT I KNOW NOW

My "plus one" is grief.
Can you set a place at your

_____

for them?

Thanks for the invitation.

I'm too sad to come.

I'm sorry I can't come to your

_____,

but grief doesn't like parties.

Can't make your

_____.

Other people's happiness is too
hard to be around.

I can't be around lots
of people right now. Want to meet
for tea instead?

Come to my

_____.

Everyone's sadness is welcome.

I'll come to your

_____

if you can give me a behind-the-scenes
job. That's easier for me to handle.

THE BEST GIFT YOU DIDN'T ASK FOR

Choose one of the gifts or new insights from your list on page 114 (or choose something entirely different). In the space below, draw or collage an image that represents this gift or insight. What "ultimate boon" do you carry with you?

When it seems like the rest of the world is uncomfortable with who you are and what you represent, hold this image in your mind. You carry necessary and powerful gifts.

PART 3

RETURN

CHAPTER 12

I Don't Want to Return to "Normal"

L oss gets integrated, not overcome.

The whole idea of getting better—or even of integrating your loss—can feel offensive, especially during early grief. For many people, their grief is their most vital connection to that which is lost. Getting better might mean that the person you lost, or the life you no longer get to live, isn't as important anymore. If you can simply move forward in your life, was your life before loss not all that special?

Use this space to write out your fears about "moving forward." If you're not sure where to begin, try starting with "If I get 'better,' does that mean losing you all over again?"

SURVIVAL AND THE PASSAGE OF TIME

The saying "time heals all wounds" is entirely wrong. Well, it's inaccurate. The passage of time isn't going to fix anything. What it will do, just by its very nature, is soften the edges of loss. Soften, not erase.

Set a writing timer. For ten minutes, explore your answer to one of the following questions:

Do you worry that time will make your loss recede into the background, like some faraway dream that never happened?

If you've had moments of feeling like you can survive your loss, did they freak you out?

Sometimes, grief makes time seem like it's frozen in place. If it feels like time has started moving again for you, what has that been like?

If you'd like a different way to engage with the topic of time, begin your writing with "Time can't erase you . . ."

LOSS OF TRUST IN THE WORLD

Some losses reorder the world; you may simply no longer believe that good things happen, or that things work out fine in the end. Losing your belief in positive outcomes is a massive secondary loss. You can't unknow what you know, and you can't unsee what you've seen.

Fill in the signs with beliefs you no longer believe.

THE PAIN ICEBERG

We often put on our "public" face when we go out, hiding private pain behind a tight mask of "I'm fine, thanks." Most of our grief remains hidden from the public eye. There is so much we do not say.

If you could tell people something, tell them what is true about grief and love and loss, something they don't know, or can't know, what would it be? What would you say if you could tell them the truth?

You might start with "What you don't know . . ." or "What doesn't show . . ." or even "Of course I've changed." Set a timer, and write your response.

PROTECTING OTHERS

ANTONIO   Will you stay no longer? Nor will you not that I go with you?

SEBASTIAN   By your patience, no. My stars shine darkly over me; the malignancy of my fate might, perhaps, distemper yours; therefore I shall crave of you your leave that I may bear my evils alone. It were a bad recompense for your love to lay any of them on you.

William Shakespeare, *Twelfth Night*

When your own stars are shining darkly over you, do you turn toward solitude, or do you chance sharing your darkness with others? Have you tried to protect other people from your pain? Have you shielded them out of love and concern for their well-being?

Do people need to be shielded from the reality you live? Set a timer and write your response.

FAMILY TREE OF GRIEF

One of us, only half-joking, said this will be a place where we medusas can take off our hats, none minding the sight of all the snakes.

Because not only can we bear the sight of each other—we crave it.

Kate Inglis, glowinthewoods.com

There is a vast divide between you and the outer world. While the divide may not always be so clear, it is now. And now is when you need other grievers: people who can look at you and truly see, really recognize, the devastation at the core of your life. Being seen changes something in grief. It helps. It may be the only thing that does.

Draw a family tree of the people you've found inside your grief, noting what they bring to you, and what you bring to them. Remember to include your online friends too.

Companionship inside loss is one of the best indicators,
not of recovery, but of survival. We need each other.

GRIEVER'S BILL OF RIGHTS

Personal relationships can get strained inside grief. To help you navigate them, here's a manifesto of relational rights:

You have the right to companionship.
You have the right to solitude.
You have the right to tell people what is and isn't helpful.
You have the right to make others uncomfortable.
You have the right to tell the truth.
You have the right to refuse all unsolicited advice.
You have the right to make decisions based on your
     own needs and on those closest to you.
You have the right to say no.
You have the right to say yes.
You have the right to ask for help.
You have the right to keep personal information to yourself.
You have the right to honor who or what you lost.
You have the right to claim your own meaning.
You have the right to sadness.
You have the right to peace of being.
You have the right to not be an "inspiration" to others.
You have the right to claim that things are horrible—or
     wonderful—and not be argued with.
You have the right to take breaks—from feelings, and from people.
You have the right to change.
You have the right to feel conflicted.

Now it's your turn. Create a personalized manifesto of relational rights in the space on the following page. Style it up. Make it awesome. Take a photo and keep it in your phone. It can be especially helpful to review your manifesto after you've had a not-so-helpful human interaction.

CHAPTER 13

Your Grief, Your Way

Grief is not an enlightenment program for a select few. No one needs intense, life-changing loss to become who they are "meant" to be. Life is not causal in that way: you need to become something, so life gives you a horrible experience in order to make it happen. On the contrary—life is call and response. We respond to what we experience, and that is neither good nor bad. It simply is. The path forward is integration, not betterment.

There are losses that rearrange the world. Deaths that change the way you see everything. Grief that tears everything down. Pain that transports you to an entirely different universe, even while everyone else thinks nothing has really changed.

You didn't need this loss so that you could learn what's really important in life. You didn't lose this just so something "more right for you" can come along. The work of transformation does not apply here. You can't just . . . act positive, find meaning, and cheer up.

You didn't *need* this. You don't have to grow from it, and you don't have to put it behind you. Both responses are too narrow and shaming to be of use. Life-changing events do not just slip quietly away, nor are they atonements for past wrongs. They change us. They are part of our foundation as we live forward. What you build atop this loss might be growth. It might be a gesture toward more beauty, more love, more wholeness. But that is due to your choices, your own alignment with who you are and who you want to be, not because grief is your one-way ticket to becoming a better person.

When you choose to find meaning or growth inside your loss, that's an act of personal sovereignty and self-knowledge. When someone else ascribes growth or meaning to your loss, it diminishes your power, subtly shames or judges who you were before, and tells you that you needed this somehow.

ON SOVEREIGNTY

Sovereignty is the full right and power that a governing body has over itself, without any interference from outside sources or bodies. You have sovereignty inside your own grief.

Sovereignty means claiming your right to be yourself, even when it upsets others. Sovereignty is the right to decide what has meaning, and what brings comfort. Only *you* have to live this, and only *you* have the right to decide what you need.

In the space below, write for ten minutes or until you feel done. Begin with "Only I have the right . . ."

NO TRUTH BUT YOURS

You know how people say things like "He wouldn't want you to be sad"? I always feel like snapping back, "Pretty sure he'd want me to tell the truth, and not lie about how I feel."

Telling the truth is powerful, even if it contradicts someone else's opinions. Sometimes, claiming your right to tell the truth feels necessary. Claiming that right begins by saying NO.

No is important.

No is a rejection of all that is not true, all that is not real.

Saying *no* is like casting a circle of protection around what is most true, claiming it as yours.

There's such a big focus, at least from the outside, on finding beauty in grief, or finding some sliver of positivity to hold on to. If you're not reaching for happiness, people seem to think you're not trying hard enough. You're not really allowed to say what's true without someone else jumping in to say you shouldn't feel that way.

Saying *no* is important. Telling the truth is important. There is no truth but yours.

To play with both no and the concept of your own sovereignty inside grief, set a timer and begin writing with the phrase "There is no truth but mine . . ."

Let your response fill these pages.

STRENGTH, NOT SACCHARINE

A whole team of cheerleaders telling you how strong you are is not terribly helpful. Being strong is often code for not letting your loss bother you, or for keeping a stiff upper lip. "Stay strong" is a weird thing to say to a grieving person.

But you do need strength—strength to survive another day when you wish you would just stop waking up. Strength to hold your gaze on the love that remains instead of dissolving into bitterness or hate. When *you* name your strengths, you get to choose how those strengths apply, and what they mean.

Use this page and the following page to draw or collage your strengths. What do you carry with you in your grief that helps you survive?

BEING GRATEFUL

Gratitude is another one of those things people outside your grief tend to use as a weapon:

> *Stop being so sad! You have two other children. You
>   need to be grateful for them.*

> Or, *Other people in the world have to deal with war or some other kind
>   of violence on top of their grief. Some grieving people don't even have
>   a place to live anymore! Be grateful that you have what you have!*

> Or, *You should be grateful; at least you had love like
>   that. Some people never get to experience it.*

Used like this, gratitude is just shame dressed up in flowing holier-than-thou robes.

That other people have it worse does not mean you have no right to pain. That you love and cherish the people you still have in your life does not make it okay that someone important is missing.

Like beauty and meaning, gratitude is a companion inside grief, not its solution. Use the space on the following page to map out the things for which you are grateful . . . on your own terms.

If you see gratitude as a companion, does it change how you feel about claiming it?

KINDER EYES

Sometimes judgment is an inside job.

Look at those bags under your eyes! And those wrinkles! Grief has aged you. You know this would be a lot easier if you just ate better and went to the gym. How can you sleep all day?! The person you lost would love *to have a day like this, and here you are wasting it!*

Whoa.

You are so damn hard on yourself, shaming yourself for not getting grief right.

Most people are way harder on themselves than they'd ever allow anyone else to be. Since we're ending a chapter about claiming truth for yourself and honoring your strengths, let's try one more thing. It's not going to be easy.

On the next page, paste in a photo of yourself or draw your likeness.

Label the parts of your face, your body, and your mind *as though you are someone you love*.

Instead of labeling the wrinkles around your eyes as hideous, horrible, ugly things that show how sad you are, you might draw an arrow and write "hard-earned wrinkles that channel tears away from my eyes so they can keep flowing." With a label pointing toward your head, you might write "an intelligent brain working overtime trying to make sense of all this."

When (not *if*) you get stuck, ask yourself, What would I see if I looked at myself with kinder eyes?

CHAPTER 14

Sidestepping Bad Support

E ven with the best of intentions, other people's "support" can feel anything but supportive. Platitudes and cheerleading come from all directions. Rude, insensitive, dismissive comments are unfortunately the norm. Most people don't mean to be cruel, they just haven't learned better ways to be supportive.

But just because they don't know better doesn't mean you have to grin and bear it.

The exercises in this chapter encourage you to express your inner snarkiness around all that unhelpful help, and give you tools to help you clarify and enforce your boundaries with people who don't get it (or don't want to).

A NOTE ON BEING NICE

We don't tear into people when they say insensitive things. We don't point out how unhelpful or mean something is, even when it's flat-out rude. Why? Because we're being "nice."

The word *nice* has an interesting history.

Nice has twelfth-century French and Latin roots that mean "foolish" and "ignorant"—literally, to be "without knowledge." Being nice means not saying what you know to be true, because the truth would upset the social order. Being nice means you silence yourself, rather than make others uncomfortable. Being nice means you let rude comments slide, so the rude person doesn't have to feel bad about their comment.

Set a timer and write your response to these two questions:

What do I gain by being nice?
What do I lose by being nice?

You can be kind, but you don't have to be nice.

ARE YOU STUCK?

I'm often asked what to do when a friend or family member seems to be "stuck" in their grief. My response is always the same: "What would 'not being stuck' look like to you? What are your expectations?" For most people, "not being stuck" means that the person has gone back to work, has regained their sense of humor, attends social events, doesn't cry every day, has put all the photos of their person away, and is able to talk about things other than their loss or their grief. They seem . . . happy again.

We think "happy" is the equivalent of "healthy," as though happiness were the baseline, the norm to which all things settle, when we're living as we should. In short, "back to normal" is the opposite of "being stuck," and getting back to normal (happy) should happen fast.

When you think of grief as an experience to be tended and not as a problem to be solved, getting "stuck" in grief might look very different.

On this page, draw, collage, or write what "stuck in grief" looks like to the people around you. On the following page, draw, collage, or write what it might look like for you.

THE PLATITUDE CHECK

Not sure if what someone said should actually feel as wrong as it does? Try running it through the "platitude check" below. Pop their statement into one of the blank spots and see how it sounds with the second half of the sentence.

> At least you had him as long as you did . . . so stop feeling so sad.
> They're in a better place now . . . so stop feeling so sad.
> Now you get to see how strong you really are . . . so stop feeling so sad.
> It wasn't meant to be . . . so stop feeling so sad.

. . . so stop feeling so sad.

. . . so stop feeling so sad.

. . . so stop feeling so sad.

. . . so stop feeling so sad.

. . . so stop feeling so sad.

. . . so stop feeling so sad.

THE VOMIT METRIC

Have a decision you need to make? When should you clean out their closet? Should you move or stay put? Change jobs, start a relationship, put their photos away, stop wearing your rings? There's so much unsolicited advice and opinion floating around the grief world that it's easy to lose track of what you actually want for yourself.

Other people's anxiety shouldn't force you to make decisions you aren't ready to make. No disaster will befall anyone if you leave your person's shoes by the door (no matter how anxious it makes someone else).

The "vomit metric" is a great tool for making decisions: if the thought of doing something makes you feel sick, now is not the time. There's no such thing as too early or too late when it comes to grief. You will do what you need to do when you need to do it. Not a moment before. It might never feel good, but if it makes you feel sick, now is not the time.

Sort any decisions you have to make—or feel like you're *supposed* to make—using the vomit metric. Which things make you feel sick? Which ones don't? If a decision feels neutral, place it in the middle.

For most things, you can take your time.
Don't let other people badger you into doing things you aren't ready for.

THE THINGS YOU CAN'T KEEP

An heirloom breaks, moths get into your person's sweater, a distant relative makes a claim on something, or you simply run out of room. No matter how much you may want to, you can't always keep all the things that remind you of the one you've lost.

On this page and the following, attach photos (or draw sketches) of things you had to give or throw away. Write a few sentences about what each object means to you.

> A PLACE TO
> KEEP THE THINGS
> I CANNOT KEEP

SHOULDN'T YOU BE OVER THAT BY NOW?

Oh, I know—you've tried to tell people about grief. You've tried explaining that "Everything happens for a reason" is a crappy thing to say. You've tried defending your right to be sad when your neighbor insists you should be over this already. You've even tried compassion. But the whole smile-and-nod thing just seems to make the grief advice flow faster.

Some people won't get it. It's not that they *can't*. They just *won't*. Your words aren't ever going to make it through to them.

Your grief, like your love, belongs to you. No one has the right to dictate, judge, or dismiss what is yours to live. That they don't have the *right* to judge doesn't stop them from doing it, however.

Because even the best defense won't stop judgment from happening, if you want to stop *hearing* said judgment, you'll need to clarify your boundaries. You'll need to make it clear that your grief is not up for debate. And then, you'll need to walk away from the argument or conversation altogether.

While doing this is certainly easier said than done, here are the steps:

CLEARLY AND CALMLY ADDRESS THEIR CONCERN	CLARIFY YOUR BOUNDARIES	REDIRECT THE CONVERSATION

These three steps, when used consistently, can significantly reduce the amount of judgment that makes it to your ears. You'll be able to sidestep the judgment-wielding madman like a grief-aikido master.

Here's how this process might look in actual practice.

Let's say you've been arguing with someone about grief for an hour. Or, rather, you've been defending your grief. Let's get you out of this.

First, acknowledge their concern: "I appreciate your interest in my life."

Second, clarify your boundaries: "I am going to live this the way that feels right to me, and I'm not interested in discussing it."

Steps 1 and 2—addressing their concerns and clarifying your boundaries—are often combined in one statement: "I appreciate your interest in my life. I'm going to live the way that feels right to me, and I'm not interested in discussing it."

Clarifying your boundaries can be especially effective when you follow your statement with step 3, redirecting the conversation (aka changing the subject): "I'm happy to talk about something else, but this is not open for discussion."

This sounds wooden and strange, I know. But the message here—including the formal wording—is that you have a clear boundary, and you will not allow it to be breached in any way.

If there are people in your life who won't accept such a clear boundary without further argument, you can stick to a stock phrase, such as "That isn't a topic I'll discuss," and then move the conversation on to something else.

If they can't leave your grief alone, you can end the conversation completely—walk away, or say goodbye and hang up. The important thing is to not allow yourself to be drawn into battle. Your grief is not an argument. It doesn't need to be defended.

It's awkward at first, but clarifying your boundaries and redirecting the conversation will become easier the more you practice. Eventually, the people in your life will either get the message—not that you don't have to be over it, but that you aren't willing to discuss it—or they'll leave. Even those people who seem immovable and permanent will fall away eventually, if they can't get on board with your boundaries.

Grief will absolutely rearrange your relationships. Some people will make it through with you, and some will fall away. Some who you thought would always be by your side will disappear entirely. People who were at the periphery of your life might step up and support you in ways you didn't see coming.

If the people in your life can handle—or even appreciate—you staying true to your own heart, then they'll make it through with you. If they can't, let them go—gracefully, clearly, and with love.

MY PET PHRASES

You don't have to defend your grief. When someone is being a jerk (on purpose or not), a handy phrase or two can redirect the conversation, or remove you from it altogether.

Use this space to brainstorm things you'll say when someone tries to draw you into battle. When you've come up with some good stock phrases, take a photo with your phone so you always have your comebacks ready. Remember, the goal isn't to win, it's to keep yourself out of pointless arguments.

CHAPTER 15

Friends and Allies and Asking for Help

While it's true that some people can be utter jerks, most people really do want to help.

It's hard to see someone you love in pain. It's an intense combination of helplessness and love that makes people desperate to make things better for you. They want you to be okay.

You don't need advice, though. You don't need solutions. You don't need to be cheered up. You need someone to see your grief, to acknowledge it. You need someone to hold your hand while you stand there in blinking horror, staring at the hole that was your life.

Companionship is everything.

This chapter will help you help others. When you don't have the energy to educate well-meaning friends and family, the tools in this chapter can do it for you.

Asking for help isn't easy for most people, so color the image on the next page to help you ease into it.

BRAINSTORMING THE PRACTICAL (AND THE WILDLY IMPRACTICAL)

Write out all the ways you could use help—from friends, family, therapists, doctors, even random strangers. Be as wild or demanding as you'd like. Freely asking for everything *here* lets you discover things you might not think of if you're being entirely "practical" or trying not to need too much.

Once you've filled the page, go back through what you've written and circle things you can ask for when people say, "How can I help?" You could even assign a color to each potential helper, and use their color to signify who might do what task.

THE "HOW TO HELP ME" PAMPHLET

Most people *do* have good intentions, it's just that the stuff they do is unhelpful at best, and rude or dismissive at worst. They need a little help to know what's actually helpful.

But you're grieving. It's not like you have a lot of extra mental energy to educate people on how best to support a grieving friend. You might not even know what you need, so how are you supposed to tell someone else?

Pass this handy pamphlet to friends and family members who want to help you. That way, you don't need to expend any of your energy explaining why "At least now you know what's really important" is not a helpful sentiment.

Be sure to check out the "I don't know how to help" boxes on the back of the pamphlet and add specific things friends and family members can do to help you. You might add things like "Take the recycling out to the curb on Tuesday nights," or "We'd love kid-friendly meal delivery a few nights a week." Give your teams tangible suggestions.

Fill out your special requests, then cut out the page, photocopy it, fold the copies in thirds to make them pamphlet shaped, and pass them around. You can also download a slightly larger version of this pamphlet to print out (see the resources section at the back of the book for the link).

If you really want your people to give you gold-star-level support, tuck a copy of "How to Help a Grieving Friend: 11 Things to Do When You're Not Sure What to Do" inside the pamphlet. It's available with the other online resources.

One last thing: I made downloadable mini-education cards, for those times you don't really want to get into it with someone but they need some redirection (see the resources section at the end of the book).

I WANT TO HELP MY GRIEVING FRIEND.

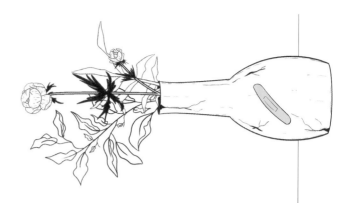

Wonderful!

It's hard work supporting a grieving person. It's hard to see someone you love in so much pain. Whether you're a casual acquaintance or an "emergency contact"–level friend, this little guide will help you deliver the love and support you most want to give.

BUT I DON'T KNOW WHAT TO SAY!

No one knows the perfect, right thing to say to someone who's inside grief. There is no one perfect thing. Nothing you say or do will make someone's grief go away—and that's okay. Grief isn't a problem to be solved, it's an experience to be tended. What your friend needs most is your love and support, your listening ear, and your willingness to show up (no matter how awkward you feel).

You can say things like:

I'm sorry this is happening.

or

I'm here, and I'm listening.

or, simply

This sucks.

HERE AFTER

here-after.com
@hereaftersocial

This pamphlet © Megan Devine
For more resources, visit here-after.com

I DON'T KNOW HOW TO HELP.

Here are some specific requests from your grieving person. Ask about—or better yet, offer to do—things that aren't on this list. (Be sure to get permission before you take action.)

- Set up meal delivery
- Have groceries delivered
- Deal with trash, compost, recycling
- Walk the dog and/or tend pets, livestock, garden
- Housecleaning
- Handle childcare or playdates
- Pick up prescriptions
- Offer transportation to/from _____
- Help me research _____
- Deal with accounts or creditors
- Help with the memorial/funeral
- Host a gathering
- Come with me to _____
- Screen my calls and texts

I WANT TO MAKE
THEM FEEL BETTER.

I'M AFRAID TO
DO THIS WRONG.

WHAT CAN I
DO OR SAY?

We don't handle grief very well in this culture. We're not really sure what to do, so we do what we've been taught: we look on the bright side. We try to make people feel better. We give them advice. We try to cheer people up because we think that's our job. We're not supposed to let people stay sad, right?

Unfortunately, no matter how good your intentions, cheering someone up won't work. In fact, trying to do so can make your friend feel worse.

It seems odd, but the way to truly help someone is to let them have their pain. Let them tell you how much this hurts, how hard it is, without you jumping in to clean it up, make it smaller, or make it go away.

Your job, should you choose to accept it, is to bear witness to something beautiful and terrible—someone else's pain—and to resist the very human urge to fix it or make it right.

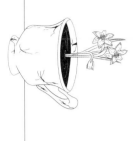

Please remember that by simply wanting to be supportive, wanting to do the hard work of loving someone inside their pain, you are doing good things.

Grieving people would much rather have you stumble through your imperfect support than have you say nothing. It's okay to be awkward. Awkward is fine. You don't have to be perfect, just present.

Here are some facts about grief:

- Grief is a healthy, normal response to the loss of someone (or something) you love.

- That grief feels bad doesn't make it bad. Grief is not an illness or a problem to be solved.

- Grief lasts a lot longer than you think. It's not over after six weeks or six months or even six years. Grief lasts as long as love lasts.

- Each person's grief is unique. Just as no one relationship is the same, no one grief is the same.

- Most of the things we *think* we're supposed to say to a grieving person actually cause more harm than good.

Here are some options:

- Share a memory. Don't avoid talking about the person who died.

- Avoid questions such as "How are you?" and "How are you *really*?" A better question is "How is today?" or "What would feel soothing tonight?"

- Put reminders for birthdays, holidays, and anniversaries in your phone. Send your friend a message on those days.

- Don't wait for just the big dates to send a text. Tell your person that you're thinking of them on any random day.

- Hang out with your friend, even if they don't want to talk. Your companionship means a lot.

- Leave them care packages. Snacks, flowers, little gifts—they all matter.

- It's okay to show up and say, "I have no idea how to do this, but I'm here and I love you, and I'm willing to feel helpless if it means you feel loved."

- Offer tangible, reliable support.

THANKS FOR YOUR CONCERN

When you're grieving, it's common for others to assess your emotional health. Not sure how to get well-meaning friends to stop worrying quite so much? Hand them a "thanks for your concern" card! Working together, choose a random word or emoji that can serve as a secret code for how you're feeling. That way, when friends ask you how you're doing, you can send them the code—and you'll both know what it means.

Cut along the dotted line to remove the facing page. Photocopy both sides of the page onto card stock, then cut out and share the individual cards with people you love.

Use these code templates with or without the physical cards:

Our secret code for "I'm okay right now" is _____.

Our secret code for "Let's go somewhere and not talk about this" is _____.

Our secret code for "OMG this sucks! I could use support" is _____.

Our secret code for "Emergency! I need help" is _____.

Watching someone suffer is hard.

Thanks for sticking by me.

Watching someone suffer is hard.

Thanks for sticking by me.

Watching someone suffer is hard.

Thanks for sticking by me.

Watching someone suffer is hard.

Thanks for sticking by me.

Watching someone suffer is hard.

Thanks for sticking by me.

Watching someone suffer is hard.

Thanks for sticking by me.

I love that you check on me, and sometimes
I don't have words to answer. Let's make it easier.

Our secret code for "I'm okay right now" is

_____ .

Our secret code for
"Let's go somewhere and not talk about this" is

_____ .

Our secret code for
"OMG this sucks! I could use support" is

_____ .

Our secret code for "Emergency! I need help" is

_____ .

I love that you check on me, and sometimes
I don't have words to answer. Let's make it easier.

Our secret code for "I'm okay right now" is

_____ .

Our secret code for
"Let's go somewhere and not talk about this" is

_____ .

Our secret code for
"OMG this sucks! I could use support" is

_____ .

Our secret code for "Emergency! I need help" is

_____ .

I love that you check on me, and sometimes
I don't have words to answer. Let's make it easier.

Our secret code for "I'm okay right now" is

_____ .

Our secret code for
"Let's go somewhere and not talk about this" is

_____ .

Our secret code for
"OMG this sucks! I could use support" is

_____ .

Our secret code for "Emergency! I need help" is

_____ .

I love that you check on me, and sometimes
I don't have words to answer. Let's make it easier.

Our secret code for "I'm okay right now" is

_____ .

Our secret code for
"Let's go somewhere and not talk about this" is

_____ .

Our secret code for
"OMG this sucks! I could use support" is

_____ .

Our secret code for "Emergency! I need help" is

_____ .

I love that you check on me, and sometimes
I don't have words to answer. Let's make it easier.

Our secret code for "I'm okay right now" is

_____ .

Our secret code for
"Let's go somewhere and not talk about this" is

_____ .

Our secret code for
"OMG this sucks! I could use support" is

_____ .

Our secret code for "Emergency! I need help" is

_____ .

I love that you check on me, and sometimes
I don't have words to answer. Let's make it easier.

Our secret code for "I'm okay right now" is

_____ .

Our secret code for
"Let's go somewhere and not talk about this" is

_____ .

Our secret code for
"OMG this sucks! I could use support" is

_____ .

Our secret code for "Emergency! I need help" is

_____ .

ASKING FOR HELP IS HARD

What's it like for you to ask for help? If you're like most people, it's not easy. Remember that your friends *want* to help. They want you to let them love you, in the best ways they know how. It's okay to ask for what you need.

Color in the message below. Draw, doodle, or collage all around it. Take a photo. Keep it in your phone, or set it as your wallpaper, to remind yourself to lean on the love around you.

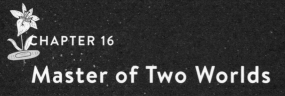

CHAPTER 16

Master of Two Worlds

T here is no going back. There is no moving on. There is only moving with—an integration of all that has come before, and all you have been asked to live.

Living with grief means going back and forth over the bridge between what was *before* and what is *now*. In time, you'll make a home inside this new world, but you don't just say goodbye to the life that was, never looking back. That's not how humans work.

Survival in grief lies in finding the connection between these two worlds.

In truth, we can hold on to nothing—not the physical world, not feeling states, not even our own thoughts. But love . . . love we can carry with us. It connects what is now to what was to what is to come. It allows us to travel between worlds.

ON MEMORIES

Especially in early grief, we replay events and memories in our minds, desperate to hold on to them. We've lost so much. We're afraid to lose what little we have left: the things we remember, the inner pictures of our life before. At the same time, there are things we wish we could forget: the image of our person suffering, or the last argument we had.

Memory can be complicated.

Set a timer and write about your relationship with memories. Begin by writing "I want to remember . . ."

You might alternate that with "I need to forget . . ."

Let your memories fill the page.

WHAT ARE YOUR TREASURES?

Draw, collage, or note things you hold most dear: snippets of memory, the first time you met, the sweetness of your morning routine, the way they told jokes at odd times. What things would you store in this treasure chest?

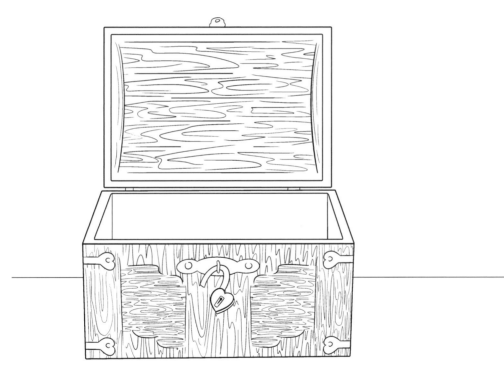

COMPANIONS, NOT REPLACEMENTS

So much of grief support (and even just everyday life) involves the "Yes, but" response: *Yes, they're gone, but you should be grateful. Yes, you're sad, but the sun is shining. These flowers are so pretty—don't they make you feel better? You've got so much that's good in your life now, why are you still thinking of them?*

Beautiful things don't replace other things. Moments of happiness or pleasure don't negate other feelings. Life isn't a swap meet where we trade one thing for another. Instead, we might consider these moments and feelings as companions:

> The ripple of light across a field of flowers lies
> beside the emptiness you feel.
> The laughter of someone you love sits alongside your sadness.
> You're glad your friend has a new baby, and it makes
> you so angry that yours is still gone.

> Life isn't either/or, it's both/and.

Use this space to write and draw the word *and*, or draw or write all the things that companion you inside your grief—whatever *and* means to you today.

BEAUTY AS AN ALLY

When all feels lost, we can still look for beauty. The presence of beauty doesn't magically remove all pain, but the absence of beauty makes things a lot harder to bear.

Beauty can be a great ally: it gives you something to hold on to when the world feels overwhelmingly dark or sad.

Use these pages to collect small beautiful things from your day: a conversation you overheard, a newly opened flower, the shape of birds in flight, random heart shapes you found in rocks or in the clouds. Write, draw, or tape things directly to the page. Beauty exists, even here in your grief.

A SLEUTH FOR SADNESS

Living what you've lived, you carry knowledge that not everyone has. You know what it's like to move through one world with part of your heart in another.

Here's a neat practice for when you're out in the "normal" world: without being weird and creepy about it, watch for signs that someone is carrying some kind of deep loss. Listen for cues. Look for the places the deeper world shows through, in the cracks, in the subtlety of the everyday moment.

It's not that you have to take any action. It's enough to notice. In your mind, you might offer love and kindness to the person. Use what you notice as a cue to soften your own gaze, to open your own heart. Who knows, you might add to the available compassion in the world. We can always use more.

Fill in the comic on the following page with the message you might silently send when you recognize someone in pain.

DO YOU HAVE TO REACH ACCEPTANCE?

A friend's husband drowned while they were on vacation. Six years on, she wrote, "I'm struggling with acceptance. Not just the acceptance of his death, but the acceptance of what my life is now, acceptance of the regular feelings of sadness and aloneness, acceptance of what is."

Acceptance is another one of those words that's often used as a weapon when people are grieving: You have to *accept* that they died. You can't heal until you find *acceptance*.

Acceptance means the "action of taking or receiving what is offered." The connotation in common usage is "to take what is offered *willingly*, and without effort."

That's a tall order. You don't have to accept what's happened. I don't know how people even suggest it's possible. Some things are unacceptable.

I wonder if instead of acceptance we looked toward admission as a more achievable goal. *Admission* can be defined as "letting in," or "acknowledging." That seems much more kind to me.

Letting in a feeling state, without attaching a bigger story to it, is a useful tool here, and it can make a big difference. For example, when you feel a familiar, deep loneliness circle back into your heart, your acceptance-focused thoughts might go something like this:

> I'm so tired of feeling this. I wish I could just accept that he's gone.
> My life is empty, and might be forever. I don't want to be lonely
> forever. But he's gone. What else is there? I wish I could accept this.

Acceptance might suggest you try to stop feeling lonely. It presents a mythic, unattainable feeling state that would be yours if only you would accept what is given—willingly.

Who is willingly lonely? No one, that's who.

If you hold admission in your mind instead, the inner storyline might go like this:

> I feel lonely today. It's so familiar and heavy. Okay, my lonely
> self: I see you. Of course you feel lonely. I wonder what would feel
> soothing to this feeling today?

Can you feel the difference? It's not that this shift in intention—to welcome and acknowledge the reality rather than try to "accept" it away—will suddenly make rainbows appear, and make your life begin again. It's just kinder (and more realistic!) to practice admitting each feeling state, seeing it for what it is, honoring it as valid and true, and asking yourself what you might need in order to answer that feeling, honor it, or move alongside it. Admission can help you step out of any self-battle storyline that only serves to deepen the uncomfortable feeling, rather than help it abate.

Try it out. Use the comic panels on the next page to create some alternate scripts for three feelings you find hard to accept but are here nonetheless—feelings you think you shouldn't feel. Draw yourself. Stick figures are fine! In one panel, write or show an uncomfortable feeling. In the next panel, draw what you might need to feel supported in that feeling. In the third panel, write a new script to use when you notice that uncomfortable feeling arise.

Then, carry this practice with you into daily life. Try out your new scripts. See what happens.

CHAPTER 17

Freedom to Live

While it may not always be this acutely heavy, your grief, like your love, will always be part of you. Life can be, and even likely will be, beautiful again. But that's a life built *alongside* loss, informed by beauty and grace as much as by devastation, not one that seeks to erase it.

Living here, alongside your loss, won't be easy. You'll most likely survive your grief, but I want more for you than just mere survival.

If this were another kind of book, this last chapter would be the happy ending. We'd circle back to name the lessons learned, celebrate your transformation, and cap everything off with a rainbow or a sunset. But it's not that kind of book.

Instead, here in this last chapter, we need to talk about the difficult things: joy, meaning, and hope.

JOY

Joy is complicated. It's not like you can follow a few easy steps and make your way from mourning to elation (no matter what some advertisements claim). Real life is not that simple.

No one talks about the dark side of joy: How the first time you feel yourself laugh, really laugh, it brings an immediate pain to your heart. How an unexpected moment of beauty gives you a feeling of joy, followed swiftly by a crushing sense of longing for the one who saw that beauty in you, or who would most appreciate it now.

How you realize, one day, three years, five years, ten years on, that you are actually happy, and that brings a flood of tears because the one you love is not here in this happiness, and you feel guilty to have found happiness without them.

Joy itself can feel like betrayal.

Happiness in any form cannot, and will not, diminish your love for the one who has died. Love just doesn't work that way. It is neither fickle nor fragile. It's not threatened by joy.

No matter how unlikely (or even unwelcome) it seems, joy will return. It won't mean you're no longer sad.

Set a timer for just five minutes and, in the space below, write about one moment of joy, even if that joy broke your heart. When did it happen? How did it feel?

Both/And, Not One or the Other

Grieving people resist any notion of joy because cultural messaging says they'd have to drop their grief in order to grasp it: *You can't be sad and joyful at the same time!*

If you have to abandon your grief in order to feel joy, we're in trouble. That grief isn't going anywhere.

Joy becomes a lot more possible when it isn't seen as a trade-off with grief. You get to have both.

What's your relationship with joy? Even the idea of it? If you don't have to let go of your grief in order to grasp moments of joy, does that change things? Use the space below to write your responses. If you feel stuck, you might begin with "Joy is complicated . . ."

A Vision of Joy

Use the space below to draw or collage images of joy—whatever it means to you. If you're not in a place where joy feels possible, create an image of what a future joy might include.

MEANING

Finding meaning is sort of the holy grail of grief work—as if finding the proper meaning in your loss will solve grief once and for all.

Loss dissolves meaning. How do you go on when the one thing that meant the most to you is gone?

Meaning is one of those things only you can claim. It's not the same as finding a reason. That's different. To live a life of meaning is to find your own internal compass, and to follow it as you honor your commitments to yourself, to others, and to the world.

Here's a tricky exercise: see if you can find a common thread of meaning stretching from way back in your early years right up to now. For example, maybe as a child you stood up for bullied kids. As a young adult, you might have advocated for an underdog of some kind. Perhaps in your career, you sought out ways to serve those whose gender or race kept them from having a seat at the table. Fairness is a thread woven into all of those choices; it's been there all along. That underlying sense of meaning or commitment might have gone dark inside your grief, but my guess is it's there somewhere.

In the space below, draw a timeline of your life. What themes do you notice as you look back? What thread of meaning or commitment runs through all the different seasons of your life?

If you find this idea of following themes through your life interesting, there are lots of places to explore it further. Check the resources section at the end of the book for links.

How Now?

Explore what has meaning to you a bit more. In the days and weeks to come, how might you express that common thread that has run through your life? Wild ideas are welcome. You don't have to be practical with this exploration. Collage, write, or draw in the space below.

Getting to Tomorrow

You might have an interesting reaction to envisioning the rest of your life: dread. Looking ahead can be hard. How heavy that feels, all those years stretching out like a life sentence. Early on in my grief, if another grieving person had told me that at five years, or nine, or twenty their life had become wonderful, I would have said, "That's not my life. That won't ever happen for me."

Look, you *just* had this weight thrown on you. It is only partly familiar. How you learn to carry it remains to be seen. You can't possibly see years down the road right now. It's just going to feel crappy to look at the future. You can't imagine who you might be; you don't have enough information. There are things that coalesce only as you live them.

When the long view is too long, look to the day: what is here, right now, at your feet. No spark of interest or meaning has to last beyond this day.

Set a timer for five minutes. In the space below, write about what feels meaningful today. Find something meaningful around you tomorrow and write about that. And then do the same the next day . . . a day after a day after a day.

HOPE

Grief, like love, has its own timeline and its own growth curve. As with all natural processes, we don't have complete control over it. What is in your control is how you care for yourself.

Living well with grief means finding ways to stay true to yourself, to honor who you are and what has come before, while living the days and years that remain. Living well is less about what you'll do and more about how you'll approach your own heart, how you'll live what's asked of you in this life.

But it's not always easy moving forward when you're not sure about the ground beneath your feet, let alone what the days and years to come might bring.

It's important, especially in such a disorienting time, to give yourself an image to live into. Something to hope for. Something that's yours. The next exercise will help you find that vision.

Imagining Your Life

Carrying love with you, moving forward as opposed to "moving on," is a complex and complicated process. Given that your loss is not something to be fixed, what would living a good life look like? How do you live here, in a world that is so completely changed?

With this series of questions as a starting place, use the following pages to explore your own idea of what "living well" might be. What kind of life do you hope for?

> Given what you have to live, what are the elements
>   of a good life? A beautiful life?
> Knowing that the complete removal of grief is not
>   the goal, what might healing look like?
> What kind of person do you want to be, for yourself and for others?
> What do you hope for yourself?

You might answer these questions all at once to create an overarching guide for this time in your life, or you might ask yourself some of these questions on a daily basis, checking in with what feels right on that particular day. You could collage your answers to the questions, too. There are lots of ways to explore how you want your life to look.

You've never had to live this before. Be gentle with yourself as you figure it out.

The Future Ahead

It can be hard to come up with a vision for your life. Finding tangible dreams can be tricky inside grief. Let's go for your hoped-for feeling-state instead, and add a little time-travel magic. Use this page to collage, draw, or write a blessing to your future self. What do you wish for that person you will someday be? How do you hope to feel in that future life? If you're stuck, you might begin with "May you know . . ." or "May you feel . . ."

The great app FutureMe (futureme.org) lets you write and schedule letters to your later self. If you draw or collage your future blessings, take a photo of what you create and send it to your future self! If you'd like to receive blessings from other grieving people, you'll find a link for doing so in the resources section at the back of the book.

FREEDOM TO LIVE

We can't end this journal on a positive note, but we can end it on a hopeful one: this is your life.

The story of this life isn't over. There are ongoing, ever-changing relationships in your life—with grief, with love, with the person you lost, with yourself. There are adventures and hardships and gifts. Your life is still the hero's journey.

At your core, you're free. Free to live this life in a way that honors your heart, honors your loss, and honors all that has come before.

In a life that feels unfair and out of control (and often *is* unfair and out of control), you are free to choose your response. This isn't some pop-psychology "make the best of it" nonsense. Choosing how you respond is about claiming your right to live in accordance with yourself. It's about claiming your own sovereignty. It's about living this life in alignment with your own sense of meaning or direction.

Your job is to tend to yourself as best you can, leaning into whatever love, kindness, and companionship you can find.

Surviving grief is an experiment. An experiment you were thrown into against your will, but an experiment all the same. There is nothing to do but to keep exploring the road ahead, carrying your love, and your loss, with you. May joy, meaning, and hope arrive to join you along the way.

Let's end this book with one last love note to you. The message on the facing page is something to carry with you as you continue to explore this life you didn't see coming. This closing message is also available as an audio download; you'll find the direct link under the resources section at the back of this book.

Several blank pages close out this journal. Use this space to write, draw, and explore your response to this closing message, or to write your own version.

*W*e come to ourselves in softening, in tenderness, to become available to pain and to love. To make our hearts available. Yield, don't fight. All is not well, and here we are with that. So we show up as tenderly as we can. Show up with tenderness for what is, softening into it. Yield.

Grief does not show you that you've lost your way. Grief is the way. Softening your heart is a radical act. Wanting for yourself something beautiful and gentle and kind. Holding out your hands to see what comes. Holding out your heart as a place for meeting what has already come.

What is here now is *love*: it's not here to make it better, not here to make grief go away, not here to give you a reason. It's just here.

And love sits beside you now, even when you don't feel it, even when it seems to have disappeared from sight. Maybe love is still here with you in whatever form it can take: a love that goes beneath everything. It makes no sense. I don't think it tries to. But there is love beneath and around and within everything.

And maybe this love knew, maybe love was there preparing you as best it could for what was to come, for what is now. Maybe you have been companioned all along, through this whole life, by love in all its forms, and at all times.

As you breathe into this space, you feel a gentleness come into you now, rising up to meet you, surrounding your heart, holding your hands. Infinite love. Infinite tenderness.

Love is with you here. A love that is heartbroken for you, as much as it is heartbroken with you. Beside you, exactly here. And you breathe in all the love that's available. All the gentleness. Meeting pain with love, we open into love.

And we come back again and again, making that choice to be present, to feel it, to receive even this—even this. All is not well, and here you are with that.

What began in love continues here along this road, on this path here.

May you know love.

May you know kindness.

May you be free from suffering.

And may you have hope in the continual, continuing experiment: to believe in a love that doesn't save you, but is still your shelter and still your home.

May what you've found in this book help you carry what is yours to live.

Acknowledgments

I don't know if I would have liked this book when my life first went sideways. When the whole world feels wrong, even the best resources can feel wrong too. I hope what I've created here would feel beautiful and useful to that person I was all those years ago.

I'm honored to have access to the stories of thousands of grieving people through my Writing Your Grief course and my social media platforms. To my writing students and my readers, thank you for sharing your grief with me. Your love for yourselves and for those you've lost shines through your words. I write with you in mind.

Jayne Agena, my wonderful patrons, and the rest of the grief revolution street team gave invaluable suggestions in the early stages of this book. My dear friend and colleague Dr. Jessica Zucker gave much needed moral support and input and, when necessary, reminded me that I can, in fact, do hard things. My agent, David Fugate, was, as always, my voice of reason. Dr. Samantha Brody provided outlets for my sarcasm and snark and acted as my quality control officer. Maika and Zee kept things running at our grief revolution HQ so I could step away to enter the long process of crafting this book.

All of these folks made this book possible. Thank you.

Thank you, as always, to my team at Sounds True, and to Naya Ismael for her illustrations. Together, we made something lovely.

I'm writing this last part of the book with a very exuberant puppy at my feet. Matt and I adopted our dog together many years ago. They've both been gone for so long now. A blink and an eternity. Joy does come around again, in different forms, at different times. To whatever it is that makes this so, thank you. Thank you for everything.

Resources

Support Organizations

Note that organizations that support people in grief, rather than pathologize it, are still in somewhat short supply. As we open new conversations about the realities of grief, new support services will emerge. There *are* good ones out there for lots of different losses, such as the examples below. Keep searching until you find something that feels right.

Speaking Grief (speakinggrief.org) houses the PBS documentary of the same name, as well as resources to help us get better at grief.

The Compassionate Friends (compassionatefriends.org) community provides support for parents after the death of a child.

The Dinner Party (thedinnerparty.org) is a worldwide community of twenty-to-thirty-somethings who have lost a parent, partner, child, sibling, or close friend.

The Dougy Center (dougy.org) provides support and resources (including grief workbooks for teens and information/ resource packets for schools and for grieving families).

Modern Loss (modernloss.com) offers beautiful essays by people grieving a variety of losses.

The International Suicide Prevention (ISP) Wiki (suicideprevention .wikia.org) is a worldwide directory of suicide prevention hotlines, online chat rooms, text lines, and resources (including resources for teens and LGBTQIA communities).

Soaring Spirits International (soaringspirits.org) offers peer support and resources for widowed folks.

The Trayvon Martin Foundation (trayvonmartinfoundation.org) offers emotional and financial support to families who have lost a child to gun violence.

Tools, Tips, and Further Education

Completed legal documents are like love letters you write for your people. They can help clarify decisions and reduce conflict (which reduces your unnecessary suffering, even if it doesn't remove your pain). For practical, real-world advice, checklists, and tips to complete the end-of-life-planning stuff—things like wills, advance care directives, and management plans for digital accounts—that everyone avoids but really needs to do, read Chanel Reynolds's book, *What Matters Most*, or visit getyourshittogether.org.

For detailed self-care strategies and cool empathy training tools, visit Kate Kenfield's website, katekenfield.com.

If you enjoyed following the threads of meaning through your life in the exercise in chapter 17, there's lots more to explore with the sparketype assessment from my friend Jonathan Fields. Find it at goodlifeproject.com/sparketypes.

If you're a therapist, medical professional, or first responder, and you'd like to learn how to better support grieving people, check out the current training resources at here-after.com.

There are wonderful books out there on dealing with trauma, for both survivors and practitioners. For a selection of current favorites, visit here-after.com/readinglists.

Downloads and Online Galleries

You'll find printable downloads of all the cut-out-and-share elements of this journal at here-after.com/journal. The closing love letter is available as an audio download, which you can find at this same link.

For the online galleries of love notes to grievers, grief mentors, and personified grief, check out here-after.com/galleries.

Key to Puzzle on Page 63

```
F L E K N S G U B K O I C T R E E A H X S R Y
P T E A D O J L I A W F O U N D H E A R T S A
E S U P P O R T T E F A O K N I G W B C V E L
V L U E R D X M L K E M H N E O P N J S E T C
O T V H I N E O A P S I E W S D N T U Y X B M
M H R S E P M N T L C L W L K R O I L F C L E
I T S O K A Y T H A T Y O U R E N O T O K A Y
S D L R U L C M E T S W Q Y C S I D B I E N C
B C E I G W B C L O T V Y A T U Z N E R K J
J S E L U E R D X T U Y T R O S R D R X N E U
U Y P K O I C T R U S U W C L Y N J C W I T F
L F M P W G W B L D A J S E T E G U W H C F E
R L O N I P N J P E P M U N S A H I N E M O S
B V R O L N T U B S A D W S H R L E T W L R C
L M E M O R Y F O B U A H M N S O P N J K T Y
K O I C V G E E W H J R U E R D X C V H I N E
I G R I E F V S F S O K V H I C E X R L E P M
E E T W Y G E C E R S H R S E P T U E R O X T
D P N J O U R S S I R U T R L E A W H I N V D
R C V H U O L L C E B M O I C T W R S E P M E
E W S D N W N E X R C O N N E C T I O N A Z P
T R E E S E P M U E R R I M H R S E P M N T S
```

About the Author

Megan Devine, LPC, is an author, speaker, and grief consultant advocating for emotional change on a cultural level. Her book *It's OK That You're Not OK: Meeting Grief and Loss in a Culture That Doesn't Understand* is considered required reading by grievers and professionals alike. Together with her team, she facilitates a growing catalog of courses, events, and trainings to help grieving people and those who wish to support them learn the skills they need to carry pain that cannot be fixed. For more, visit here-after.com.

About the Illustrator

Naya Ismael is a Syrian self-taught illustrator who works in both digital and traditional media. Both of her parents are artists, and she fell in love with art at a very early age, spending her childhood watching her parents work in their studios and going to art galleries. Her work includes digital murals, book covers, user interfaces for mobile apps, logos, and apparel, and she participated in the first digital art gallery in Damascus, Syria. Naya is studying marketing at the Higher Institute of Business Administration in Damascus. See her work on Instagram @naya.ismael and on Behance @nayaismael.

About Sounds True

Sounds True is a multimedia publisher whose mission is to inspire and support personal transformation and spiritual awakening. Founded in 1985 and located in Boulder, Colorado, we work with many of the leading spiritual teachers, thinkers, healers, and visionary artists of our time. We strive with every title to preserve the essential "living wisdom" of the author or artist. It is our goal to create products that not only provide information to a reader or listener but also embody the quality of a wisdom transmission.

For those seeking genuine transformation, Sounds True is your trusted partner. At SoundsTrue.com you will find a wealth of free resources to support your journey, including exclusive weekly audio interviews, free downloads, interactive learning tools, and special savings on all our titles.

To learn more, please visit SoundsTrue.com/freegifts or call us toll-free at 800.333.9185.